A Training Manual for Americans With Disabilities Act Compliance in Parks and Recreation Settings

A Training Manual for Americans With Disabilities Act Compliance in Parks and Recreation Settings

by Carol Stensrud Ed.D., C.T.R.S., R.T.R.

Venture Publishing, Inc.
State College, PA

Disclaimer

The author and publisher caution the professional to be sensitive to the abilities and limitations of the participants. This book does not, in any way, guarantee compliance to the ADA law. It is the responsibility of the agency and individual service provider to fully understand the ramifications and requirements of the ADA law per specific setting and consumer needs. Professional judgement on your part is required.

Printed in the United States of America

Production: Bonnie Godbey
Printing and Binding: Rose Printing Company, Inc.
Manuscript Editing: Michele L. Barbin

Library of Congress Catalogue Card Number 93-61009
ISBN 0-910251-63-0

10 9 8 7 6 5 4 3 2 1

A Sincere Thank You

To those who so generously contributed to the
development of this book:

Dr. John McGovern, Dr. Stuart J. Schleien, Dr. John Rynders,
Ms. Amy Stein, Ms. Sharon Adams, and Ms. Terry Murray.

And to the many unnamed, who have influenced my work
over the past decades.

About the Author . . .

Dr. Carol Stensrud, C.T.R.S., R.T.R., Ed.D., is an Associate Professor of Recreation and Leisure Studies at California State University, Sacramento and a practicing certified recreation therapist.

Her professional interests have long been focused on the 'non-clinical' side of therapeutic recreation. She has founded several grant projects, agencies, and training programs directed at integration, understanding, and inclusion of individuals with disabilities.

Stensrud directs LEISURANCE Associates, a consultation and training firm that provides keynote addresses, workshops, and seminars as well as training materials, such as books and tapes for public and professional groups. Topics include: *The Leisure and Wellness Connection, Power of Leisure, Is There Life After Work?* and *Free To Follow Your Bliss: The Americans With Disabilities Act and Leisure Settings*.

Her writing and speaking style is unpretentious and often humorous. However, her intent is serious. Stensrud finds satisfaction in the new impetus that ADA legislation lends to the promotion of leisure fulfillment for ALL—a long sought goal in her career. She emphasizes there is still much to be done.

She wishes you the very best of success as you embrace this new law and hopes this manual will be put to good use in the process of welcoming individuals with disabilities.

Table of Contents

Chapter 5 Program Planning _____93

Chapter 6 Common Disability Categories ____117

The Beginning Chapter

Introduction

WELCOMING individuals with disabilities was born out of necessity. The newly enacted and landmark legislation, the Americans With Disabilities Act (ADA), calls upon all people involved in recreation and leisure services to welcome and include individuals with disabilities in their programs.

This manual is intended to be a guide for staff training about providing integrated leisure services for individuals with disabilities. The focus is on the real face-to-face leadership concerns of staff and program planners in public recreation and leisure services. It could also be useful for not-for-profit, and private recreation ventures as well.

What will this manual do? Assist you in a user-friendly manner in planning and implementing staff training programs related to the Americans With Disabilities Act. Meaning—we are getting ready to meet and greet people with disabilities!

What this manual will not accomplish: *Provision of complete information on compliance issues related to the ADA, nor a guarantee of compliance.*

This manual is one of many tools to be used as part of an ongoing process leading to good faith accommodation.

Definitions

A few informal definitions:

Americans With Disabilities Act (ADA): Public law 101-336 is civil rights legislation intended to eliminate discrimination against individuals with disabilities in all aspects of American life including employment, transportation, communication, public services, and accommodations provided by state and local government, and private entities. The ADA was enacted in 1990, and enforcement began January 26, 1992 (104 STAT 327-378).

Americans With Disabilities Act, Title II, Local Government: A section of the ADA that protects qualified individuals with disabilities from discrimination in services, programs, or activities of all state and local governments.

Americans With Disabilities Act, Title III, Public Accommodations and Commercial Facilities: A section of the ADA that prohibits discrimination against qualified individuals with disabilities in private entities providing public accommodations. This includes commercial and nonprofit businesses. Private clubs and churches are not included unless they provide public accommodations such as a child care center.

Qualified Individual With A Disability: An individual with a disability who meets the essential eligibility requirements for your programs and services (45 CPR 84.3).

Disability: With respect to an individual, a person that meets one of three tests defined in the law, is considered to be an individual with a disability for purposes of coverage under the ADA. The law states an individual with a disability means one who:

      a. has a mental or physical impairment which substantially affects one or more of the major life activities of that person; or

      b. has a record of such an impairment; or

      c. is regarded as having such an impairment (Section 35.104 definition 28 CFR Part 35 Federal Register, DOJ, February 28, 1991).

Compliance: Following the regulations set forth by the ADA.

Good Faith Efforts: Learning about the ADA and taking sincere actions related to following its directives.

Most Integrated Setting: Defined in the ADA as the delivery of service in an environment that maximizes interaction between individuals with and without disabilities.

Reasonable Accommodation: Taking steps to welcome individuals with disabilities. These steps include but are not limited to: providing accessibility modifications, changing policies and procedures, acquiring necessary auxiliary aids, adapting communication methods and promoting increased consumer relations through advisory board input, staff training, and technical assistance.

Unconditional Positive Regard (UPR): Holding personal values that display acceptance of all individuals regardless of their ability, skill level, or disability.

Consumer: For the purpose of this manual, the term 'consumer' will refer to a qualified individual with a disability.

Generic Programs: Those programs and services offered by agencies to the general population.

How To Use This Manual

This manual is a source and guide for trainers. It is sequentially developed in short chapters that build upon each other. Each chapter could stand alone as a training session. Overheads and copies of selected pages may be made for use in training sessions. A variety of exercises, questions, and discussions are provided in each section designated by the following symbol:

Additionally, this manual is designed to be easily understood and could be provided to staff members as required reading.

Since the level of experience or understanding of the learner or trainee is unknown, the author has made the decision to start from the beginning, so—

LET'S GO!

Getting Organized For Staff Training

All members of your agency need some type of training and sensitization to the ADA. Administrators, supervisors, direct service providers, advisory board and commission members, volunteers, bus drivers, janitors, and all types of support service personnel make up the total environment that welcomes individuals with disabilities. This manual focuses on the training of supervisory and direct service providers.

Plan For Planning

1. *Appoint a person to be responsible for the ADA training.* This person should have some experience with individuals with disabilities. A therapeutic recreation specialist who has a background in community recreation would be ideal. A Certified Therapeutic Recreation Specialist (look for the letters C.T.R.S., or R.T.R. after his/her names) should be considered as a consultant who would oversee and assist in training. See Chapter 7—Resources (page 145).

2. *Allow time for planning.* Plan a schedule that is reasonable. Allow at least three hours of preparation for every hour of actual training.

3. *Develop a training task force.* Gather the support of interested staff and community members. Elicit expert help. People with disabilities and/or staff of local advocacy groups (e.g., United Cerebral Palsy, Association of Retarded Citizens, Head Injury Foundation) are invaluable for input on disability issues. See Chapter 7—Resources (page 145).

4. *Develop a schedule for training.* Decide what your priorities are, and make a timeline that will outline those topics. Fit training times into your agency's schedule and coordinate the times to suit staff needs. Training is mandated and usually paid for in one way or another. A 'day away' or retreat is often much more effective than two-hour meetings during the workweek that may be missed. A creatively planned, cost-effective 'retreat' may be of greater benefit because of the 'intensity' provided for learning.

5. *Schedule facilities for training.* Arrange for a meeting space as soon as possible. Consider such things as: length of meeting, number of participants, space for activities, and length of time facility is required.

6. *Acquire training support materials.* There are many types available such as audio visuals, speakers, books, articles, and adaptive equipment for demonstration. See Chapter 7—Resources (page 145).

7. *Record training sessions.* Video recording is widely available these days, but audiotaping may be much more useful for homework training, and future transcribing. *Video tips:* Many communities now have a not-for-profit function of cable television that allows community groups private use of video equipment, studio productions, and even editing functions as well as training. Call your local cable company for information. Additionally, video equipment may be rented through various sources in your community. Your local college or university instructional media center may be of assistance also.

8. *Develop a learning center.* This could be a collective effort by geographic region, like a city or county, and might be cooperatively funded. Include books, videos, films, and other materials that could be used as resources for staff. A computer-interactive, independent learning program about the ADA would be fantastic. This could be a job for your next intern.

9. *Think team training.* Each division of your agency needs to become responsible for servicing all consumers. Encourage staff from all departments to become involved so that the training can be delegated to a team in the future.

10. *Involve consumers.* The best way to learn to welcome individuals with disabilities is to learn from persons with disabilities. Seek advice and speakers from a variety of advocacy groups on training and implementation plans. See Chapter 7—Resources (page 145).

11. *Network.* Many agencies may be sponsoring training in your area about the ADA and related topics. Contact them and suggest cooperative efforts. Local colleges and universities may have therapeutic recreation classes that focus on community recreation and disability awareness. You may call upon this valuable resource for a variety of assistance: (1) direct staff training, (2) recorded classes or video materials, (3) handouts, or (4) as a source of continuing education classes for employees to either take for credit or audit.

A Basic Training Plan

1. Evaluate existing services and identify areas of your agency that are affected by the ADA.

2. Involve others. Ask community advocacy groups and other leisure professionals to help evaluate the services your agency provides for individuals with disabilities, and identify priorities for training.

3. Evaluate staff and determine what they need to know.

4. Identify the main point of the training session. Ask: If the participants learn only one thing from this session, what should it be?

5. Organize information to aid participants in understanding the ADA.

6. Anticipate the reactions participants may have, and prepare to answer questions.

7. Prepare a summary of the major points.

8. Conduct training sessions.

9. Implement plans identified in training sessions. Do something every day. Start right away. Be willing to break old habits. Learning a new behavior may be awkward; that's OK. This is the first step toward growth. Do something you wouldn't have done before the training.

10. Follow up. Staff training only BEGINS when training sessions are finished. Involve others in this process. Encourage the trainee to ask: How am I doing with my training implementation plan? What specifically have I done differently since my training? What is my next step?

11. Stick to it. Learning happens in steps. Keep learning objectives clearly in focus. If your learning plan is not successful, adapt and adjust it. Practice new skills until it feels natural to use them.

12. CONGRATULATE AND REWARD YOURSELF FOR PROGRESS.

A Basic Training Session Outline

1. Grab attention with a poem, a picture, a story, or a question.

2. State the main point of your training session.

3. Present information to aid participants in understanding the ADA and inclusions of individuals with disabilities.

4. Allow for learner interaction. Simulations, games, exercises, demonstrations, checklists, or any other positive learning experience that allows *input* on the part of the learner is useful.

5. Use multimode communication: Verbal lecture is only *one* way to get the point across. Use video and audiotapes, songs, stories, visual aids, props, equipment, games, puppets, and other action-oriented activities to get the message across.

6. Ask for and answer questions.

7. Check for understanding by asking questions.

8. Summarize major points.

9. Ask the trainees to apply what they have learned by developing specific action plans. Make the list of things to do *short*, so it is easily accomplished.

10. Thank participants and creatively reward them for attending.

11. Make it fun! Do be aware that training need not be boring! Cartoons, small tokens or rewards for coming, refreshments, and colorful handouts all assist in learner motivation.

2

The Law—ADA Focus: Title II

This chapter will provide a brief background of the Americans With Disabilities Act (ADA) and then jump right into:

- ADA's Broad Purpose, Scope and Inclusion

- Five Major Sections of the ADA

- The ADA "Shall NOT Dos"

- The Shall Dos of the ADA

- Enforcement

The Americans With Disabilities Act (ADA)

Before we delve into the law, let's talk.

Exercise Time!

Respond to the following questions (or statements):

1. What recreation and leisure experiences have contributed to your well-being and to helping you to be all that you can be?

2. How would you be different (in mind, body, and spirit) if those recreation and leisure opportunities were denied you. For example, what if you had no vacations, camping trips, boy or girl scouts, birthday parties, athletics, singing or music lessons, and no chance to go to the playground. Who would you be today?

For 43 million individuals who live with disabilities, the opportunity for recreation and leisure experiences that contribute significantly to personal development have been unavailable (ADA, 42 USC 12101, July 26, 1990).

Thus, the Americans With Disabilities Act (ADA) has been passed after many long years of advocacy and struggle by a large and broadly represented consumer group who, like you, wanted equal access to all of life's pleasures.

And now to the law...

The Americans with Disabilities Act (ADA) was signed into law on July 26, 1990. The adoption of the ADA comes after twenty years of effort by individuals with disabilities and advocacy groups, to remove the barriers to full participation in *life*. Actually, the law was not new in concept. Previous federal legislation mandated nondiscrimination against individuals with disabilities in publicly funded services since the mid-1970s. The law was a landmark in several respects, as follows:

1. Broad Purpose

TO ELIMINATE DISCRIMINATION AGAINST INDIVIDUALS WITH DISABILITIES AND WELCOME THEM INTO ALL WALKS OF LIFE.

2. Broad Scope

The ADA, in its entirety, applies to (a) publicly-funded services (local, county, district, state and federal), for example: City Parks and Recreation; (b) not-for-profit services or agencies (nonprofits), for example: YMCA; and (c) private for-profit enterprises (commercial enterprises), for example: Disneyland. The requirements of the law vary with the size and type of agency.

3. Broad Inclusion

The question of who qualifies under the ADA is answered in the legal text as follows: "A person is considered to be disabled if: they have a mental or physical impairment that substantially limits one or more major life areas (35.104)." Life areas include, but are not limited to: caring for oneself, seeing, hearing, walking, daily living skills, learning, and working.

The term physical and mental impairment include, but are not limited to: contagious and noncontagious diseases, orthopedic, visual, speech and hearing impairments, cerebral palsy, epilepsy, muscular dystrophy, multiple sclerosis, cancer, heart disease, diabetes, mental retardation, emotional illness, specific learning disabilities, human immunodeficiency virus (HIV) related disease (symptomatic or asymptomatic), tuberculosis, drug addiction and alcoholism (if in recovery) (45 CFR 84.3). The following conditions are NOT covered by the law: some sexual behavior disorders (e.g., exhibitionism), compulsive gambling, and illegal use of drugs (28 CFR 35.131).

Practically speaking, the ADA applies to almost everyone who would be considered to have a disability. In addition to the conditions that are generally thought of as disabilities, the ADA adds coverage to these: individuals who have a record of a disability, individuals who are regarded as having a disability, even though they may not, and individuals who may face discrimination due to their relationship with persons with disabilities.

To the point, the ADA is a civil rights law that is intended to protect individuals with disabilities from discrimination.

Five Major Sections Of
The Americans With Disabilities Act

Title I. Employment

Employers may not discriminate against individuals with disabilities in the workplace. This includes all employment actions (e.g., hiring, firing, promotion).

Title II. Public Entities

Local and state government agencies must not discriminate against individuals with disabilities. All government facilities (federal, state, and local), services, public transportation and communications must be accessible to individuals with disabilities and must meet the requirements of Section 504 the Rehabilitation Act of 1973 (28 CFR, 35.130).

Title III. Public Accommodations

All public businesses, and private, commercial and not-for-profit agencies are prohibited from discriminating against individuals with disabilities in any program or service. Public transportation provided by a private entity is covered in this title.

Title IV. Telecommunications

Public and private entities must make all services accessible to persons with communication impairments.

Title V. Miscellaneous Provisions

Agencies and areas that do not fall under the previous titles as well as some technical and legal issues are included in this section. Federal wilderness areas fall into this section.

These are the broad provisions of the ADA. Title II, which is directed at publicly-funded recreation and leisure settings, is covered in more detail in the next section.

The Americans With Disabilities Act
"Shall NOT Dos"

Title II of the ADA which concerns recreational settings includes a list of SHALL NOT DOS related to discrimination. The law states...

"NO QUALIFIED INDIVIDUAL WITH A DISABILITY SHALL, ON THE BASIS OF DISABILITY, BE EXCLUDED FROM PARTICIPATION IN OR BE DENIED THE BENEFITS OF THE SERVICES, PROGRAMS, OR ACTIVITIES OF A PUBLIC ENTITY, OR BE SUBJECTED TO DISCRIMINATION BY ANY PUBLIC ENTITY (28 CFR 35.130)."

WOW! That is quite a statement. Essentially, this means that whatever services you provide must be available in a useful and welcoming manner to any qualified individual with a disability that requests those services. This includes lessons, clubs, trips, swimming, camping, playgrounds, equipment rental, training, tests, licensing, certificates, day care, referrals, and health screening. Everything from the public relations to registration, consumer program planning input, to the actual 'fun and games' must be available to all consumers.

YES! A MAJOR SWITCH OF PERCEPTION IS GOING TO BE NEEDED.

THE WORLD IS EVERYONE'S PLAYGROUND!

NOW WHAT? The law helps clarify what we are not to do. Here are a list of SHALL NOT DOs with examples provided for each.

Eight Shall NOT Dos[1] of
The Americans With Disabilities Act

1. Thou Shall Not Provide Unequal Opportunities For Individuals With Disabilities.

This means that all services should be available to all consumers. Segregated recreation programs are still permitted, but they can no longer be the standard or only option. If a person using a wheelchair wants to play golf, he/she need not be limited to a special handicapped golf program that is available only at one site, once a month. All individuals have the right to choose from the whole universe of opportunities in leisure. Special recreation times are generally very limited in scope and opportunities are very restrictive. A person with a disability has the right to choose a segregated or special type of program, but he/she also has the right to choose to participate in an integrated program as well.

This means that EVERY program you offer needs to gear up to welcome people with disabilities OF ALL TYPES.

2. Thou Shall Not Provide Opportunities Which Are Less Effective.

If a consumer enters a program, he/she is legally entitled to quality services of an equitable nature. Token programs will not work. If a child with mental retardation has not mastered the basic swimming lesson level I, then options need to be explored in order for him/her to gain the benefit proposed. Does he/she need to take the class again at reduced fee? Does he/she need ten minutes of private instruction during a group lesson? Does he/she need a leisure buddy to help reinforce his/her learning experience? What will it take to ensure effective lessons for him/her?

---

1. All Shall Not Dos from (28 CFR, Subpart B General Prohibitions Against Discrimination on Section 35.130 ADA Federal Registar February 28, 1991)

3. Thou Shall Not Provide Separate Services For The Person With A Disability Unless It Is Necessary.

The concept of the most integrated setting or least restrictive environment (LRE) comes into play here. This basically means that a person needs to be integrated into an environment that is the norm, unless he/she cannot benefit from this setting.

Now the important question is...

Who decides? The consumer will decide initially. If a person wishes to enroll in regular tennis lessons and he/she happens to use a wheelchair, what should be done?

Now, just as would be done with anyone without a disability, the person's skill level should be evaluated so that he/she could be referred to the appropriate skill groups. If a person, with or without a disability, signs up for an advanced course and evidences, over time, less than advanced skills according to your predetermined skill level checklist or test, then he/she should be referred to the appropriate skill level group until such time as he/she can meet the advanced level skill requirements.

What about the child who has a behavior problem in the swimming class? Would it be better to give him/her private lessons? Is swim class only about learning to swim or is there more to the experience? The benefits must be looked at from all sides. What are the goals and objectives of the service?

One example of appropriate separate services is home-based services for those who are unable to travel. This has been done for years by some selected parks and recreation agencies and nonprofit agencies. A person who cannot travel to a service must be provided equal access to the service.

4. Thou Shall Not Aid or Perpetuate Discrimination By Furthering Relationships With Groups or Organizations That Do Discriminate.

This suggests that other organizations that cooperatively sponsor events, share facilities, or purchase from or contract to your agency must be evaluated in terms of the ADA. If a group, club, organization or individual is not making good faith efforts to comply with ADA and they contract or have formal relations with your agency, then your agency is at risk of being out of compliance with the ADA. *This means that if the annual banquet for the local soccer association is held at your facility, and that association does not allow kids with disabilities to play on their team, your agency may be at risk of a lawsuit for perpetuating discrimination.*

5. Thou Shall Not Exclude Individuals With Disabilities From Serving On Your Advisory Board or Any Other Official Committee Of Your Agency.

It would be wise to elicit membership of consumers with disabilities on committees to show good faith and gain from their expertise.

6. Thou Shall Not Select A Site For Development Of A Facility or Recreation Area That Cannot Be Made Completely Accessible.

Example: Your program offers a day camp on a rugged terrain island every summer. This is the only day camp you offer. The boat ride nor camp programs are accessible to a child using a wheelchair. What to do?

Several options are available. The camp could be moved to an accessible site, or an additional section of camp could be offered at a more accessible location. Alternatively, a voucher to attend another camp of similar quality sponsored by another agency could be offered while yours gears up for accommodations. A mixed program could be offered where some of the camp time is spent at the nonaccessible site, yet the experiences are provided to the child with a disability via video and other simulations and approximations of the experience (like rock climbing). The child who uses a wheelchair may not be able to go to the island this year, but could be introduced to rock climbing via video and/or climbing wall. Then he/she could be offered a basic rappelling experience in an area that is accessible.

This example shows the various options related to access issues, including:

1. Acquire a new and accessible facility;

2. Move the program to an accessible site; and/or,

3. Provide the experience through alternative programming methods.

At least one third of all experiences offered by your agency should be accessible now. Then as time, transition, and remodeling continues, all facilities should become accessible.

New federal access guidelines called the Americans with Disabilities Act Access Guidelines (ADAAG) have been developed. For ongoing programs, a facility self-evaluation is required by the ADA. This includes identifying architectural barriers and planning for removal of the barriers. See Accessibility (page 103) for additional information.

7. Thou Shall Not Discriminate In Administration Of Tests, Licensing or Certifications That Your Agency Sponsors.

This includes CPR classes, first-aid classes, water safety courses, and fishing licenses. What if a person with a visual impairment came to take the test? What adaptations would be necessary for a person who could not physically complete a leg splint, but wanted to become certified in first aid? The accommodations that public schools and colleges have made for students with disabilities in regard to taking exams and proving competency will have to be considered. Some examples of accommodations are providing a reader, and a transcriber, extending time limits, and providing large print exams.

8. Thou Shall Not Charge Higher Fees For Individuals With Disabilities.

For example—A program costs $40 per person. An interpreter is needed for the individual with a hearing impairment to participate. Extra fees to cover the cost of the interpreter cannot be charged to the individual with the disability. *This means that the cost of the interpreter has to be spread over all participants, not just the participant needing the extra service. Alternatively, fundraising could be done to establish an accommodation fund to be used as needed.*

The Shall Dos Of
The Americans With Disabilities Act

or Reasonable Accommodation In Parks And Recreation Under The ADA Title II

What about the Shall Dos? They are designated as reasonable accommodations in the law.

Because of the variety of recreation and leisure settings, the ADA is general enough to apply to all settings. Each and every requirement is not spelled out in detail. Agencies must take actions to assure that REASONABLE ACCOMMODATION IS AVAILABLE.

The following ADA provisions give guidance on compliance with the requirement of providing reasonable accommodation. Some examples of each provision are provided. These provisions are not all inclusive. The provisions include but are not limited to:

1. Thou Shall Change Rules, Policies, and Practices.

Example: Parks that do not allow dogs must allow service animals to accompany individuals with disabilities. Another example: If your agency previously had a first come first serve program sign-up process with long lines, a call in reservation time, or FAX registration may have to be added for a person who cannot mentally or physically tolerate standing in line. In the extreme, some agencies have had a policy to not allow individuals with disabilities (in general, or with a specific type of disability such as Alzheimer's) to participate in the programs. This is a *highly* discriminatory policy that MUST be changed [302 (b) (2) (A) (ii) of Title III applied to Title II settings].

2. Thou Shall Remove Architectural Barriers.

Adapt existing facilities, relocate programs and/or build new facilities that are accessible. Be creative in making programs accessible to all consumers via telecommunications, homebased, or other adaptive methods. Example: A community beach party is not accessible to individuals who use wheelchairs. A plastic carpet can be purchased to be rolled and placed on the sand to create a firm path for wheelchairs. This would allow consumers who use a wheelchair to come down to the beach and play. Another example: An annual fundraising event features dancing on a platform accessed by stairs. A ramp could be built for the platform (per access guidelines), or the concept of the platform could be abandon for the event. This part of the law speaks to all aspects of an event, not just widened doorways in the bathroom (35.149-159). See Accessibility (page 103).

3. Thou Shall Remove Communication Barriers.

The law requires that appropriate steps be taken to ensure that communications with individuals with disabilities are as effective as communications with other individuals with or without disabilities. Telecommunication Device for the Deaf (TDD) and relay services for persons who do not use voice are available to meet the needs of consumers who have communication impairments. Acquire a TDD for your high demand registrations. Make all public relations communications available in alternative formats such as braille or audiotape. Fire safety adaptations such as light and wind signals for individuals with hearing or visual impairments should be installed in your facility (35.160-164). See Communication (page 64) and Public Relations (page 107).

4. Thou Shall Remove Transportation Barriers.

Work to assure equal access to any program where transportation is provided by your agency, such as sporting teams and field trips. Contract with or purchase accessible vans. Arrange public transportation to suit program needs. Advocate for cooperative community based accessible transportation systems that suit all consumer needs. If a consumer is unable to locate accessible transportation to your agency, it may be necessary for your agency to provide transportation, even if transportation is not provided for consumers without disabilities. Provide home visits to those who are unable to travel due to their disability or lack of accessible transportation. Example: A Saturday program for teens is a drop-in type program with no registration required. Regularly the teens are taken to special community events in your nonaccessible vans. John, who uses a wheelchair, attends one Saturday. A wheelchair accessible van should be available for immediate rental. Another approach would be to require advanced registration. This would give your agency the time to reserve an accessible van in advance. Alternatively, all participants could use the public transit system in your area, provided that it is accessible (Section 224 PL 101-336 Title III 35.130, 35-150).

5. Thou Shall Provide Auxiliary Aids and Services.

Auxiliary aids and services include adaptive equipment and supplies needed to make equal access available to all consumers. This may include assigning extra staff, providing sign language interpreters, and securing qualified readers. It is most efficient to ask consumers what types of accommodations or adaptations they need. Begin to acquire adaptive equipment such as assistive listening devices, tandem bikes, kayaks, and pool flotation devices. Example: An adaptive lift for a pool is expensive, complicated, and requires two staff members for operation. Current consumers may be served as well with portable, removable, transfer steps positioned at the shallow end of the pool. These can be used independently or with the assistance of one person in most cases. Consumers should be consulted to determine exact needs before expensive purchases are made.

Various levels of accommodation are indicated for various situations. The law indicates that the expressed need of the individual with a disability should be the primary consideration when selecting the most appropriate auxiliary aid or service. There is always room for mutual discussion and resolution. Example: A person with a hearing impairment requests an interpreter for the drawing class. Since the class is primarily instructed by demonstration, the instructor and potential class members come to the agreement that the first two introductory classes be interpreted by a certified interpreter. After that, daily written instructions, outlines of materials, and visual demonstrations would be reasonable accommodation. During the final class, discussion and review of each class member's work is required. An interpreter should also be employed for this session. Over time, the class instructor may become motivated to learn basic sign herself! (35.160)

6. Thou Shall Provide Services In The Most Integrated Setting.

First referral to a recreation program must be to generic programs and services that are open to everyone, unless the consumer indicates otherwise. If a person with a disability is participating in a generic program, he/she may be referred to a segregated setting only after accommodations, and adaptations have been tried, documented and retried. Example: A potential customer who has some motor impairment indicates interest in art classes. Explain the registration procedures and determine if he/she meets your generic entry requirements for the class. Ask if he/she needs any special accommodations. Accommodate him/her in the generic class. Do not assume that he/she wants an adaptive art class unless he/she states this. (35.150)

The Majority Of Individuals With Disabilities Will Fit Into Generic Programs

SPECIAL RECREATION will have it's place, but it will not be the only place. Its nature will change also. Special recreation staff will be utilized to provide adaptive leisure skills classes and leisure education in some instances. Their expertise will be most valued in public relations, referral, registration, placement, staff training, and staff support areas. Additionally, advisory board functions, funding, community liaison and networking, and the ADA compliance issues will fall into their domain. Their responsibilities will expand from providing special and different programs to coordinating efforts to make reasonable accommodations in ALL programs and services of your agency.

Enforcement

The ADA has very strong enforcement methods. Public leisure service agencies must complete a self-evaluation of programs, services, activities, and methods of administration by January 26, 1993. Key topics of this self-study are communication, staff training, program fees, interaction, or integration. A self-assessment of facility accessibility was to be completed by July 26, 1992.

After the self-evaluation, the agency is required to develop a transition plan that identifies existing discriminatory practices, and present an outline of proposed changes, time frames, estimated costs, and responsibilities for those involved.

Complaints

The intent of the ADA is to allow for individuals with disabilities to seek reasonable accommodation—no more—no less. Each agency is asked to develop a formal ADA internal complaint system. This format provides the opportunity for consumers with disabilities to make their problems, needs and possible solutions known to the agency. An individual who believes that he/she has been subject to discrimination on the basis of disability must file a complaint within 180 days of alleged discrimination. Each agency needs to develop methods for requesting, discussing, responding and negotiating for reasonable accommodations. This system must be timely and user friendly, and is usually coordinated by the agency designated ADA officer (353.170).

Additionally, consumers can file complaints directly with the Department of Justice. Complaints will be analyzed case by case. The bottom line requirement for the public agency, if the complaint is deemed valid, is to gain compliance with the ADA.

When Do You Not Have To Comply With The ADA?

An agency is occasionally not required to comply with certain aspects of the ADA. There are several situations that are considered an undue burden, or beyond reasonable accommodation.

Undue burden will be tested by the courts, but the conditions necessary to prove undue burden are difficult to meet. The elements of the test for undue burden consist of three parts. They are:

1. Fundamental alteration in the nature of the program, service, or activity of the facility.

2. Undue economic burden.

3. Undue administrative burden.

This manual is not intended to address administrative levels of service, therefore, these issues will not be covered in-depth. In general the whole scope and nature of the services you offer should be analyzed on a case by case basis to determine if reasonable accommodations are, indeed, undue burdens. Publicly-funded agencies (i.e., those services that are paid for by tax dollars and that have the purpose of serving all people) are required to make every effort to adhere to the ADA, except in rare cases.

3

Concepts

This section will examine important concepts that are valuable to the understanding of the welcoming process. They are:

- The Leisurability Model

- Normalization

- Integration

- Eight Guidelines for Positive Interactions

- Avoiding Eight Common Problems

This brief segment will look at some of the concepts and benefits of leisure and explore the Leisure Ability Model.

Exercise Time!

Discuss the following questions:

1. What is leisure?

2. Why is leisure important?

Characteristics Of Leisure[1]

LEISURE PROVIDES A PATHWAY THAT LEADS TO THE ATTAINMENT OF DESIRED EXCELLENCE.

LEISURE INCLUDES FREEDOM OF CHOICE, SELF-MOTIVATION, PERSONAL PLEASURE, AND JOY.

LEISURE OFFERS OPPORTUNITIES FOR PERSONAL FULFILLMENT, DIGNITY, CONTROL, INDEPENDENCE, SELF-EXPRESSION, AND INNER JOY.

LEISURE ALLOWS FOR THE YAHOOS! OF LIFE.

Benefits Of Leisure: Physical, mental and spiritual well-being, self-esteem enhancement, stress management, creativity enhancement, and assistance in coping with life changes are proven benefits of leisure. Additionally, leisure offers resistance to addiction and depression, opportunities for virtue, contribution, joy, happiness, love of self, others, community, and the environment, and contributes to the overall satisfaction with life.

LEISURE EXPERIENCES ALLOW US TO LIVE LIFE TO ITS FULLEST!

People are hungry for readily available, high-quality leisure opportunities because of the immense benefits derived from them. People with disabilities seek the same quality leisure experiences as people without disabilities, yet, they have often been denied or excluded in the past.

---

1. Characteristics of Leisure adapted from Howe-Murphy, R. & Charboneau, B.G. (1987). *Therapeutic Recreation Intervention: An Ecological Perspective.* p. 5. Englewood Cliffs, NJ: Prentice-Hall, Inc.

Exercise Time!

Discuss the following questions:

1. Do all people with a disability need recreation therapy?

2. Does your agency have to provide recreation therapy? Please discuss.

Leisurability Model[2]

The answers lie in what is called the *Leisurability Model*. This model explains various types of recreation service that may be needed by consumers. Briefly explained, it consists of three parts. They are:

1. Treatment

The purpose of this type of service is rehabilitation. The intent is to improve functional ability. Rehabilitation or habilitation processes are used. The setting may be clinically-based or community-based.

Sample: John who is coming out of a coma and has paralysis. One of the professionals aiding John is the therapeutic recreation specialist (T.R.S.), who will introduce him to the therapeutic pool at the appropriate time during his rehabilitation. There he will work on his motor skills. The T.R.S. also encourages him to use poetry (one of his past interests) to express his grief and anger in an effort to assist in his adjustment. He learns to adapt his leisure skills by utilizing a head stick to operate a tape recorder to record his poetry.

2. Leisure Education

The leisure lifestyle of most people in our society evolves and develops throughout the lifespan of the individual. Leisure education services utilize an educational model which operates on the assumption that behavior can change and improve as the individual acquires new

---

2. Leisurability Model adapted from Peterson, C.A., and Gunn, S.L. (1984). "Therapeutic Recreation Service Model," in *Therapeutic Recreation Program Design: Principles and Procedures 2nd ed.* pp. 11-52. Englewood Cliffs, NJ: Prentice-Hall, Inc.

knowledge, skills, attitudes, and abilities. The purpose of this type of service is to assist a person in developing skills that allow him/her to reach full leisure potential. These skills include leisure planning, decision making, social interaction, and specific leisure performance skills. Additional skills include transportation, money management, and safety. The settings for this type of service are diverse: clinics, transitional residential settings, and community-based recreation programs.

Sample: John (from before) is about to be discharged from the hospital. He is anxious to go home. The therapeutic recreation specialist (T.R.S.) at the hospital sets up a meeting with the community recreation staff to introduce John to the newly-available accessible beach front, and adaptive scuba classes offered by the Parks Department. John is given a tour and registration interview. He returns to the hospital for his last few weeks of therapy. In his twice a week leisure education session, discussions about community acceptance, attitudes, and ways to deal with possible prejudices and barriers are the focus. His family is involved in a 'trial' beach outing with John and the T.R.S. in order to learn what he can do on his own, when to help him, and more importantly *when not to help him.*

3. Recreation Participation or Pure Leisure

The purpose of this type of service is the fulfillment of pure leisure needs. It is not treatment or education. The primary services offered are regular leadership styles, except when a modification is needed for participation access. The settings include community-based recreation of all types: public, not-for-profit, and private commercial settings. Sample: John has been home now for a year and uses a sport wheelchair. He enjoys the beach and wants to plan a trip. He calls a travel agent to inquire about accessible accommodations in Hawaii. The agent has the information he needs. He makes his plans, invites his significant other, and flies to Hawaii. When there, he visits state parks, campgrounds, luau shows, and makes his deepest dive yet with a private scuba company. He does all this because he wants to. It is his leisure.

All three components of service could be needed by a person who has a disability at some time in their life. It is not the level or degree of disability, nor where they reside that determines if a person needs treatment, leisure education or recreation participation. A person residing in a rehabilitation center who is receiving daily therapeutic recreation treatment still has the basic human need just to play and be at leisure. He/she may choose to attend a community recreation program or to stay in and order a video and pizza. It is the individual's right to choose pure leisure.

These three components of service are not separate concepts. They flow together in a continuum. A park program may join a clinical service for a joint program and interact regularly on referrals. A clinical program may use the community extensively for the leisure education process. Some community recreation programs offer facilities and programs for treatment purposes, such as the YMCA's Women with Mastectomies Swim and Support Group.

THE GOAL FOR ALL CONSUMERS IS LEISURE.

LEISURABILITY MODEL

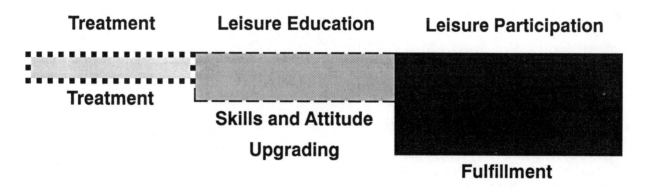

Treatment **Leisure Education** **Leisure Participation**

Treatment

Skills and Attitude

Upgrading

Fulfillment

–This is where your focus and services are valued–

Now you know something about Leisurability. This concept and continuum are important to understand as programs and services are evaluated for compliance with the ADA.

Normalization

Exercise Time!

1. Brainstorm on the elements of an adult life in your community that make up what is considered the norm, or the average experience (e.g., having access to a car/transportation, choosing where you live). Make a list and compare.

2. Discuss which of the above elements you would guess are not often easily attainable for someone with a disability?

Normalization is a philosophy as well as a guideline for service provision. It basically requests that persons with disabilities be provided the opportunity to have a lifestyle that does not mark them as different in the eyes of others. The main emphasis is *to offer consumers equal opportunities for a lifestyle that is as close to the norm as possible.*

Rules of Normalization

Examples for recreation programs:

1. Normalize Rhythms of the Day, Week, Month, Year, and Life.

People usually play in the afternoons, evenings, and weekends. They have holidays on the exact date and take regular vacations. Would an adult dance ending at 8PM be the norm?

2. Normalize Developmental Experiences.

People play, work, love, and retire in a pattern following maturity. Age appropriate activities and opportunities are key to this rule. Would Santa Claus having people sit on his knee be the norm for a group of adults with cerebral palsy?

3. Normalize Respect.

The interests, wishes, and desires of a person are honored (within reason). Choice is the key here. Planning for activities without significant input from your consumer group is to not respect their wishes. There are many examples to note a lack of respect (e.g., talking to a caregiver or relative instead of the individual with the disability).

4. Normalize Social-Sexual Opportunities.

Adolescents and adults are sexual beings and express their sexuality in a variety of ways. Beyond the bedroom, we flirt, dance, fantasize, and socialize. Just because a person has a disability, doesn't mean they are not interested in expressing their sexuality. Average, in this case, does not mean traditional. The full spectrum of sexual preferences should be honored. Does a person using a wheelchair dance, flirt, and make love? Recreation settings are often the place for socialization to take place, so agency policy on appropriate social-sexual behavior needs to be equitably implemented. Social-sexual skill upgrading classes are now offered at some parks and recreation settings. Staff members may be uncomfortable with this area. Sensitize them by providing education and opportunities for discussion.

5. Normalize Economic Standards.

The right to work, earn money, and spend money is the norm in today's world. The work ethic is tied heavily into the current value system in the United States. This may have to be reassessed as more and more people face unemployment. People may desire a chance to pay their way. Freebies are OK in some instances, but a fee (based on a sliding scale and with time payments available) allows for dignity.

6. Normalize Environmental Standards.

The right to live, play, and work in the community is critical. Community playgrounds, pools, shopping centers, and churches are some places people play. Individuals with a disability are no different in their rights or desire for full access. Living in a home called *Hope House* and going to the *Handicapped Center* fifty miles away to both work and play does not, in any way, resemble the norm. A special recreation office and segregated recreation program is not the norm.

Keys To Normalization
Related To Recreation Service Provision

Physical Integration: A chance to be close to people of all kinds, facility, and transportation access.

Use Of Generic (for Everyone) Places and Spaces:

Nonlabelistic Services: "Easy Going" Aerobic Class for individuals needing a less rigorous routine. *NOT* "*Retarded Aerobics*" for those who can't.

Social Integration and Inclusion: Sequential opportunities, and support systems such as Leisure Buddies.

Smallness: Small numbers of individuals with disabilities mixed within a group of persons without disabilities

A typical mix could represent the ratio of individuals with disabilities to those without estimated anywhere from 1:10 up to 1:17.

Age Appropriateness: The real age of the person is the indicator of what type of program or service he/she attends. Mixing wide age ranges is usually not a good idea unless the activity is intergenerational in nature. Providing children's activities to adults is *NEVER* appropriate. *NEVER!*

NOTE: The author has been asked a thousand times, "What about the 30-year-old person who has the intelligence of a 2-year-old, wouldn't it be OK then?" *NO!* It is up to the program coordinator to be creative. Is hand-built ceramics more difficult than working with Play-Doh®? It's lifeskills and image we're talking about. *How would you feel if you were offered fingerpainting?*

Upgrading of Images: Use activities and facilities that promote a positive image of individuals with disabilities. They often live with a huge stereotype.

- Why always go to fast foods for lunch when a restaurant is just as reasonable?

- Think how the person could be involved in an action or activity that would enhance his/her place in the eyes of others (e.g, volunteering, fundraising)

- Treat each person individually. A rose is not a rose. Learn about each person's individual wishes, dreams, and desires. Assist them in any way that you can in fulfilling their wishes, dreams, and desires. If a person wants to travel, get them in a Travel Club!

- Help them fit in. Show, talk, model, how to dress, participate, and make friends in recreation programs if needed. If finishing touches are missing, you could be a significant role model.

FOCUS ON ABILITY! RATHER THAN DISABILITY.

Use yourself as a check point...

If it feels weird, not fun, or stupid,

If you wouldn't be caught dead doing it,

If an individual without a disability would refuse,

If it's uncomfortable...

Then it probably is **NOT** within normalization guidelines.

Normalization information adapted from:

Wolfensberger, W. (1972). *The Principle of Normalization in Human Service*. Toronto, ON: National Institute on Mental Retardation.

Nirje, B. (1980). "The Normalization Principle." In R. J. Flynn and K. E. Nitsch (Eds.) *Normalization, Social Integration and Community Services*, pp. 36-44. Baltimore, MD: University Park Press.

Integration

The ADA states that "public entities must administer services, programs, and activities in the most integrated setting appropriate to the needs of qualified individuals with disabilities, i.e., in a setting that enables individuals with disabilities to interact with nondisabled persons to the fullest extent possible (28 CFR 35.130)."

The word integration means to bring together. When applied to persons with disabilities, it means bringing individuals with and without disabilities together. Integration is a process rather than an ultimate end. It includes the following elements:

1. Social closeness,

2. Physical proximity,

3. Dignity,

4. Choice,

5. The right to risk and fail,

6. A valued role in society, and

7. A natural system of friends, family and community members.

The implementation of an integration process could be thought of as a stream or road upon which the consumer travels. At each point along his/her travels, the individual would be afforded the opportunity to engage in age appropriate, culturally appropriate, and skill appropriate activities that are geared to meet his/her current level of social, emotional, physical, and cognitive ability.

Sequential integration is a multi-faceted process. It includes the provision of support services, particularly in the early stages. These may include skill upgrading programs and classes, additional personnel support, leisure education, and specialized equipment. Physical integration must be made possible through the provision of accessible transportation and facilities. See Accessibility (page 103). Social integration must be expedited through the education and involvement of the community.

Exercise Time!

Divide into small groups, or do this individually. You are given a task. It is as follows: You are to educate and facilitate the integration of a person from another country into American culture. You are to teach him/her to be included into a very hip health club in your town. They are to become a welcomed and valued member of the health club. The person does not know our language, customs, or have any notion or values about 'working out' or being physically fit.

What steps and actions would you take to assist this person in feeling welcome at the club? What systems of support could you develop to assist the individual to fit into the regular flow of the health club and become a valued member?

You have a one-year period within which to plan your educational process. You have as much money as you need. For the actual exercise, you have 15 minutes.

BEGIN!

Take a few notes, and share your strategies with others.

You can see that integration is an intricate process.

Let's look at two models of integration that will help you understand the flow and process of integration.

Integration NOW Concept

by contributing author: Ms. Sharon Adams

Integration NOW is like the freeway of life. Each level represents a type of road or integration.

Level I 'Frontage Road.'

This is where a participant runs parallel to the freeway. Segregated special recreation programs may be in Level I. These types of programs rarely intersect with generic recreation. They may have the same view and direction, but a slower pace and more stop lights.

Level II 'Merging Traffic.'

This level allows participants to merge or integrate into the mainstream or generic recreation program, but the pace is adapted. Support services such as additional staff and adaptive techniques or a charge in rules may be utilized.

Level III 'Middle Lane.'

This is where participants are really in the regular flow of the program, but on occasions, need to go to the slow lane or even exit for awhile. Support services may also be called for.

Level IV 'Fast Lane.'

This is where the participant and others feel comfortable with very few adaptations. Of course, at times a change in lane or level might be desired by the participant.

This analogy makes sense when we look at integration of persons with disabilities. A person just released from the hospital with a head injury may need to start on the frontage road in a special recreation leisure education program. Another person with a head injury of ten years may already be speeding down the fast lane by competing in a team triathlon or attending a concert with a loved one.

The key to integration is providing a view that looks all the way down the road of opportunities. No one is forced to stay in the slow lane forever. Putting better fuel and wheels under the person in the form of experience, leisure education, and needed support services, allows everyone his/her rightful place in his/her chosen lane of life.

Sequential Recreation Integration Streams

Here is another integration stream. This one was invented twenty years ago by Dr. Stensrud. It is called sequential recreation integration streams (see figure, page 36).

Some discussion about the words used:

Developmental Educational Techniques: Step-by-step teaching processes utilized to teach a leisure skill to a person. Example: The ultra-careful swim class for people afraid of the water, where you begin by just getting adjusted to the water at the side of the pool.

Back Door Integration: When people without disabilities come into a more segregated group of persons with disabilities to provide the beginning of peer integration. Example: A special recreation boy scout troop invites the generic scouts to join them on various camping trips. This is sometimes called reverse integration.

50-50 Integration: This is where the number of individuals with and without a disability closely assume a half-and-half mix. Examples: An intramural sports league with 50-50 mix, or a tandem cross-country skiing group for persons with visual impairments. One-to-one leisure buddy systems are a prime example of this type of integration in which one person with a disability is matched with a person without a disability to participate in leisure activities.

Fully-Integrated or Front Door Integration: This is when a person with a disability walks in the door of any activity he/she chooses. He/she fits within the average mix of persons with and without disabilities, a ratio of one to about ten.

Source of Motivation: You can see that from specialized to transitional to fully-integrated services, the source motivation for the activity begins to change. At the specialized level, the motivation and leadership often comes from the therapeutic recreation specialist. At the transitional level, it changes to the recreation specialist as accommodater/encourager in cooperation with the consumer. At the fully-integrated level, the client is in complete control with very little outside motivation needed.

- -

Sequential Recreation Integration Streams
by Dr. Carol Stensrud

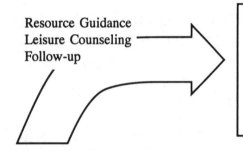

Resource Guidance
Leisure Counseling
Follow-up

FULLY-INTEGRATED SERVICES
Normalized Area of Society

1) Private, Public or Commercial
2) Client Directed
3) Fully Integrated
4) Normal Techniques

TRANSITIONAL SERVICES
Programs "With" Disabled

1) Community-Based
2) Client and Recreation Specialist Directed
3) Fifty-fifty Integration
4) Developmental Educational Techniques

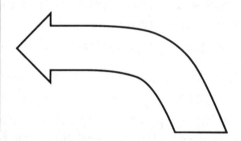

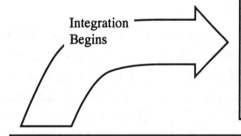

Integration
Begins

SPECIALIZED SERVICES
Recreation Programs "With" the Disabled

1) Community or Clinic-Based
2) Therapist Directed
3) Back Door Integration
4) Developmental Educational Techniques

THERAPEUTIC RECREATION

1) Institutional Setting
2) Therapist Directed
3) Segregated
4) Therapeutic Techniques

KEY

1) Setting
2) Source of Motivation
3) Type of Integration
4) Techniques Used

Integration Techniques—Moving Toward The Free-Way!

1. Emphasize *Ability First!*

2. Utilize generic, nonlabelistic environments: the parks, swimming pools, malls, and playworlds of the person without a disability.

3. Promote age appropriate activities.

4. Promote peer interaction between all participants.

5. Allow for the person with a disability to adjust to new people, new environments, and new experiences.

6. Teach for success! Similar to your challenge to have the person from another country feel welcome, the person with a disability, due to a variety of life experiences, may not know how to fit in. We all want to fit in!

7. Think total picture: clothing, style, manners, money management, social skills, travel and safety skill, and leisure skills are part of fitting in.

8. Allow for a level of individuality. We don't want to be clones.

9. Be an advocate, one who promotes *integration*. Work with consumers, parents, care providers, advocacy organizations, and your own staff and administration to enhance their belief that it works.

10. If the program is at a segregated or special recreation level, ask the question, "Where do persons with disabilities go from here, and how can I best assist them in getting there?" The ADA makes "special and different" illegal in most instances.

11. Think small. Small groups or one individual with a disability can assimilate successfully into a community center, club, or class. A large group that exceeds the average ratio makes for a difficult situation and often leads to failure.

12. Leisure buddies are very useful in the integration process for some consumers. These are volunteers (usually, although some may be paid staff) that are matched with consumers with similar interests in order to help the person get into the swing of things and coparticipate. Leisure coaches are volunteers

who are responsible for actual leisure skill training and lessons. Ask if your agency has a leisure buddy program or volunteers for this purpose. See Resources (page 145).

13. Community awareness training may be needed. It may not be. Experience involving persons with disabilities may be sufficient training. At other times, a brief discussion or a disability awareness program may enhance the flow of individuals into the fast lane.

Exercise Time!

1. What could you do to help program participants without disabilities better understand persons with disabilities?

2. What could you do to facilitate positive interaction between people with and without disabilities?

3. What techniques could you plan to help reduce possible negative interaction between people with and without disabilities?

MANY POTENTIAL APPROACHES ARE POSSIBLE!

The following is a summary of guidelines for positive interactions from *Together Successfully*[3] (which are found in their entirety on pages 40-54):

Eight Guidelines for Positive Interactions:

- Structure activities to aromote cooperative interactions
- Determine primary purpose of activity
- Determine desired roles of participants
- Recruit nondisabled participants
- Strengthen friendship skills of nondisabled participants
- Use a supporting curriculum
- Prepare adults to be facilitators
- Promote integration as *everyone's* responsibility

Avoiding Eight Common Problems:

- Integrating too quickly
- Using cooperative learning at the wrong time
- Age mismatch
- Lack of preparation for integration in new situations
- Lack of individualization
- Failure to take advantage of choice-making opportunities
- Sacrificing participant safety to integration
- Peers assuming adult teaching roles

3. Rynders, J.E., and Schleien, S.J. (1991). *Together Successfully.* Arlington, TX: Association for Retarded Citizens.

Eight Guidelines for Positive Interactions

■ **Guideline 1: Structure Activities and Surroundings to Promote Cooperative Interactions**

Without structuring an integrated situation for cooperative interactions, nondisabled individuals often view their peers with disabilities in negative ways, feel discomfort and uncertainty in interacting with them, and sometimes even display rejection toward them. Unless the setting is structured for cooperative learning experiences, competition might emerge and actually socialize children without disabilities to reject peers who are different in some way. What does it mean specifically to structure an activity for cooperative interactions?

One of three models of activity structure is usually applied when there is a group of people to instruct: **Competitive, Individualistic or Cooperative.** Each is legitimate and has strengths in particular situations. Furthermore, sometimes they can be combined in an activity. We shall define each of them and look briefly at some applications.

Competitive

Competition in its traditional application leads to one person in a group winning, with all other group members losing. If it is used in a group where one or more of the members have disabilities that make successful task participation difficult, it will be likely that the participants with disabilities will "come in last." An example of competitive structuring from the world of camping would be five children, some of whom have movement disabilities, lining up at the

Additional Strategies for Promoting Cooperative Interactions

- Seat participants in small integrated groups.

- If a participant with a disability has a behavior problem, have him or her become part of a larger group of participants without disabilities. Rotate the interaction responsibilities of members without disabilities.

- Arrange supplies so that everything needed by a group is in one small area rather than scattered around the room. This will help to keep group members involved with each other.

- Emphasize the importance of enjoying an activity with another person rather than the speed and/or accuracy with which it is done.

- Develop directions for the task in such a way that they require an interdependent (cooperative) effort, rather than independent or competitive effort.

edge of a lake for a canoe race. Each has a canoe and a paddle to use. The camp director tells them that the person who reaches the other side of the lake first will win a canoe paddle. It doesn't take much imagination to realize that the children with poor coordination and low muscle tone don't have much chance of winning. NOTE: Informed program leaders would not use a competitive goal structure in this manner, of course, but would rely on one or both of the following structures instead.

Individualistic

In an individualistically structured situation, each member of a group works to improve his or her own past performance. Potentially, every member of the group, including members with disabilities, can win a prize for improvement if the targets for improved performance are not set too high or are not inappropriately matched with a disability condition. Using the canoe example again, suppose that the adult leader lines the group up on the shore of the lake and tells them that the last week when they paddled across the lake each person's crossing time was recorded. Then, the adult says that each person will win a canoe paddle if he or she improves his or her time, even if the improvement is very small, Now everyone can be a winner. This structure is often used in amateur athletics where a child is encouraged to beat his or her last time or achieve a personal record.

Cooperative

Cooperatively structured activities are very helpful in many types if integrated programming, particularly if peer friendship is the goal. By its very nature, a cooperative learning structure (if handled properly) creates an interdependence because the group's attainment of an objective with everyone contributing is the quality that determines winning. Using the canoe illustration, the adult leader might have the five children climb into a war canoe (a large canoe), give each person a paddle, and tell them that they are each to paddle as well as they can and that they will all win a prize if they work together to keep the canoe inside some floating markers (placed in such a way that perfection in paddling isn't required). The adult leader will need to paddle alongside to determine that everyone is paddling, and that they are encouraging and assisting one another.

In conclusion, to promote *positive social interactions* between participants with and without disabilities, the cooperative structure will work better than the other two. Why? Because in a competitive situation, the child is concentrating on paddling the fastest; he or she doesn't have time for socialization. Similarly, in an individualistic structure, the child is concentrating on bettering his or her own past performance; again, there is no incentive for socialization. In the cooperative structure, however, each person wants to encourage every person to achieve a group goal that is realistically attainable. This promotes positive social interactions such as encouragement, cheering, and pats on the back. In a word, cooperative structuring is the best means to achieving successful integration from a *socialization* standpoint.

■ Guideline 2: Determine Primary Purpose of Activity: Skill Development, Socialization, or Both

Most activities will probably promote both skills development and socialization, but there will also be times when one objective is given priority over the other. For instance, a 4-H club leader may designate certain periods of the year primarily for project completion, such as the months preceding the spring fashion show or county fair. These will be times when participants—especially those without disabilities—will be intent on finishing their individual projects. Socializing will be minimal during these times and may even be regarded as a distraction by nondisabled 4-H members who are intent on making the "best bookshelf ever entered in the county fair." At times such as these, the leader must be clear about the intent of the activity in order to avoid creating a situation in which participants are frustrated by trying to fulfill conflicting objectives. When skill development is the focus, the program must be organized so that both participants with and without disabilities are able to pursue that objective. One option is to give nondisabled participants the opportunity to work on their own projects prior to the session with a partner who has a disability; that way they have time to develop their skills or complete their project, and also time to focus on interacting with their companions.

■ Guideline 3: Determine the Desired Roles of Participants

It is important that the leader not only be clear as to the primary purpose of the activities, but also that he or she decides the desired role of nondisabled peers in interaction with peers who have disabilities. The leader must determine whether the nondisabled peers will be interacting as **companions, tutors,** or **both companions and tutors.** Each role has a different purpose and fits well into a cooperative learning orientation.

It would seem that a peer tutoring approach is used if the primary objective is the acquisition of specific skills, or a peer friendship program is used if social interaction is the main objective. But making a choice between the two is not generally necessary.

The usual purpose of a **peer tutor** program is to have a peer without a disability teach a skill to a peer with a disability. The relationship of peers in a tutoring program can be thought of as "vertical," that is, the tutor is in charge ("I'm the teacher, you're the pupil."). A typical example of a peer tutor program is where a 12-year-old child without disabilities comes to a special class and works one-on-one on picture recognition skills with a 6-year-old child with a disability. Using a set of flash cards, the older child gives systematic word practice drill to the younger one. This is the typical peer tutoring arrangement. However, the child with a disability should not always be involved in recreational activities as the one who receives "help," often an expectation when tutoring programs are used. It is important for a child with a disability to experience a giving as well as a receiving role.

The primary purpose of a **peer companion** program is to promote positive social interactions between a child with a disability and a child without a disability. To achieve this purpose, the peers should be approximately the same age, although it is fine if the child without disabilities is one or two years older than his or her partner. It is not often desirable for the child with a disability to be older than the child without a disability; our research shows that this can create a socially awkward situation. The relationship between two people in a peer companionship program can be thought of as "horizontal," that is, a relatively equalized, turn-taking relationship. A typical application of this arrangement is where two peers, one with a disability and one without, make a pizza by taking turns putting on the ingredients (sauce, cheese, etc.) and by washing the dishes together.

How To Act As A Companion To A Peer With Disabilities

• Welcome your partner and stay close to him/her during the activity.

• Smile, talk pleasantly, and try to maintain eye-contact when talking.

• Divide up task to encourage your partner to be involved.

• Make the activity enjoyable and let your partner know you are having a good time.

• Take turns. Your partner may not be used to this, so be patient. Don't help too much or too soon. But, if he/she appears to be confused, losing interest or frustrated, step in. To assist, describe (pleasantly) how to perform the task, than invite him or her to do it. If that does not work...Show how to do the task as you continue to explain how to do it. Then invite him/her to do it like you did. If that doesn't work...Guide him or

continued...

The two peer roles (companion and tutor) raise issues for the program leaders to consider. At first, it may appear that the choice of one or the other is easy: the program or activity is tailored according to the outcome desired—skill acquisition or socialization. It would seem that a peer tutoring approach is used if the primary objective is the acquisition of specific skills, or a peer companionship program is used if socialization is the main objective. But making a choice between the two is not generally necessary. Instead, leaders can opt for concentration on the facilitation of friendship, at least initially. Then, later, it is very normalizing for one friend to teach another to play a new game, thus allowing the skill acquisition to occur in the natural course of the friendship.

■ Guideline 4: Recruit Nondisabled Participants

A helpful tool for recruitment of nondisabled participants—as well as adult volunteers—is a slide presentation that illustrates people with and without disabilities interacting in natural and interesting ways. This provides a positive image for prospective participants, many of whom may have negative mental pictures of integrated programs due to lack of exposure to persons with disabilities, stereotypes of persons with disabilities, or negative experiences with persons who have disabilities. Recruitment presentations that depict positive interactions between persons with and without disabilities help create, among potential members, the expectation that they will have a positive experience in an integrated program. Possession of that expectation alone can go a long way toward creating a successful program.

How To Act As A Companion To A Peer With Disabilities
(continued)

her through the task by gently nudging his/her arm toward it, or by actually moving your partner's hand to perform the task while continuing to explain how to do it. Then, invite him or her to do it.

• Say something pleasant about your time together as the activity ends.

If you photograph your own slides, obtain written photo-use permission for each person in your pictures (for minors or others unable to legally sign for themselves, have the parent/guardian sign). Also, inform all parents or guardians of your intent to provide an integrated program and receive consent to have their son or daughter participate. While this type of permission may not be required, it is important to do it to avoid misunderstanding.

■ **Guideline 5: Strengthen Friendship Skills of Nondisabled Participants**

Why should the adult leader spend time with instruction in friendship? Don't the children without disabilities naturally interact in a friendly way with children who have disabilities? Yes, and no. Yes, they usually know how to interact in a friendly manner (although they may need to have their usual friendship skills sharpened or expanded). And no, peers without disabilities do not often have the knowledge and skills to interact easily and ably with a person who may be different in some manner. Frequently, a disabling condition presents interaction challenges never experienced by peers without disabilities. Participants without disabilities will need instruction in how to cope with communication, movement and other types of challenges.

Meetings involving nondisabled group members and adult leaders should occur frequently, perhaps immediately before or after an integrated session. During these meetings, discussion can focus on how a particular interaction problem can be overcome, new ideas for interacting, and specific techniques that can be used during one-on-one activities (see 'How to act as a companion to a peer with disabilities' for a list of techniques). A useful exercise for these meetings is to engage participants in problem solving based on the ideas for activity modification found in Chapter Three of *Together Successfully*. For instance, they can think out loud about how to modify a pizza making task so that a child with cerebral palsy can participate with limited arm and hand use. When nondisabled peers apply themselves to figuring out how to enhance participation of a partner with a disability, it builds their empathy, self-awareness, and maturity. [For further information on activity modification in this publication, see Chapter 5—Program Planning, page 93.]

■ Guideline 6: Use A Supporting Curriculum to Enhance Knowledge of Companionship

Use of the *Special Friends* curriculum (Voeltz et al., 1983) can be helpful in enhancing the knowledge and motivation of participants without disabilities. Used for short informal group discussion periods of 15-30 minutes, these materials are often shared with nondisabled participants between interaction sessions. Suggested topics from the curriculum include:

• **How Do We Play Together?** Discuss how companions take turns, say nice things to each other, help each other out when a task is difficult, stay close to each other when playing, smile at each other, and so forth. In other words, reinforce the interaction techniques that they have been taught to apply during integrated activities.

• **How Do We Communicate?** Discuss communication tips, such as, talking slowly, allowing time for response, trying another way to communicate if your companion does not understand you, and not giving up. The use of common, simple manual signs (e.g., "hello," "good," "you," "me") can be introduced, too.

• **What Is A Prosthesis?** Discuss the use of tools (e.g., ladder, paint brush) that people without disabilities need in order to do certain tasks (e.g., paint a house). Show examples of a prosthesis (e.g., an artificial limb or adapted equipment) and explain how it is like a tool which people without disabilities use.

• **How Does A Person With A Disability Live In The Community?** Invite a person with disabilities to come and talk about how he or she travels from home to work, goes camping, etc.

• **What Is A Best Friend?** Discuss the nature of friendship. Ask participants to think about similarities and differences in their relationship with their friend with a disability and their best friend (if not the same person).

■ **Guideline 7: Prepare Adults To Be Facilitators**

An adult assuming an interaction-facilitating role will be instrumental in determining the success or failure of integrated activities. Facilitation usually takes two forms:

• Overall planning and operation of the program, including recruiting participants, structuring activities for cooperation, and preparing nondisabled peers for the integrated system.

• Facilitating cooperative interactions by modeling appropriate behavior and reinforcing groups for interacting as well.

     The following is an illustration of how a leader might facilitate cooperative interactions. Suppose that the group is engaged in an art activity. The leader could do the following:

> An adult assuming an interaction-facilitating role will be instrumental in determining the success or failure of integrated activities.

Facilitating Cooperative Interactions

During activities, adult leaders can facilitate cooperative interactions between participants with or without disabilities by doing the following:

- Prompt positive interactions when they are not occurring.

- Reinforce positive interactions when they are occurring.

- Redirect behavior if either partner gets off task or is behaving inappropriately.

- Step in if a situation is deteriorating.

• **Prompt Positive Interactions** when they are not occurring, for example, "Mary, I'll bet Jennifer would like to paint with you."

• **Reinforce Positive Interactions** when they are occurring, e.g., "Bill and Jim, you both did a really nice job with the mural." Rewarding words should not be given out indiscriminately, but should be given right after the desired behavior occurs.

• **Redirect Behaviors** if either partner gets off task or is behaving inappropriately. For instance, the nondisabled partner may become "sloppy" in his or her interactions by becoming too autocratic, too laissez faire, or sometimes too absorbed in his or her own project. Or a participant with a disability may wander away from his or her companion.

• **Step In If A Situation Is Deteriorating,** e.g., a child has a tantrum. Sometimes a child will need to be removed for a cooling-off period. The adult leader will need to gauge the seriousness of a problem situation and move in quickly if it is out of control or, better yet, if it is just beginning to get out of control.

■ **Guideline 8: Promote The Essential Idea That Integration Is *Everyone's* Responsibility**

While it is generally agreed that public and private recreation agencies must assume a leadership position in assuring equal access to their services, "key" individuals, such as group home staff members, parents, and teachers, must assist with the integration process. These individuals can be involved by helping recreation directors and activity leaders to complete environmental analyses and decide on appropriate adaptations to enhance participation in programs. They can also serve on community advisory boards that discuss efforts to assure that integration occurs, assist in recreation staff in-service training and recruit volunteers (Schleien and Ray, 1988).

Parents, especially, can play a key part in promoting integration. Susan Hamre-Nietupski and her associates bring out this point very well in an article titled, "Parents as Advocates." In the article she describes several highly practical things that parents can do to see that an integrated program becomes a reality and thrives in the community.

Avoiding Eight Common Problems

Occasionally our best intentions to extend programs to people with disabilities turn sour because we create unnecessary problems for ourselves. Eight of these common problems are discussed below, along with suggestions to help you avoid them.

■ Problem: Integrating Too Quickly

One community 4-H club voted unanimously to bring Janice, a child who has severe emotional problems, into their club. Not only did they want her to join immediately, they wanted to include her in every activity, 100 percent of the time. Their commendable enthusiasm and generosity turned to feelings of guilt when Janice soon had to be removed because the children could not cope with her inappropriate behavior. If the club leader and participants had gradually phased Janice into the program, perhaps choosing a short, largely social activity to begin with, Janice and her peers could probably have succeeded together.

■ Problem: Emphasizing Socialization At The Wrong Time

Sometimes, an adult leader in a 4-H club asks peers without disabilities to devote themselves to socializing with a peer who has disabilities at a time in the club's schedule when every member is trying to finish his or her sewing or woodworking project for entry at the county fair. To avoid this problem, during times of individualistic or competitive skill-building activity let the participant without disabilities devote their time to their projects and ask a community volunteer or sibling to come in to help the person with a disability work on his or her project. Or, alternatively, perhaps the club members without disabilities will be willing to devote a portion of their meeting time to helping the child with a disability with his or her project using a cooperative "round-robin" system. Using this approach, nondisabled peers take turns for a short period of time with a partner who has a disability, but spend most of their time on their own projects.

■ Problem: Age Mismatch

A young child without disabilities will feel socially awkward if expected to interact with a substantially older child with a disability—particularly if the interaction expectation is that of peer tutoring. A peer tutor structure works best when the tutor is considerably older (about twice as old or more) than the person to be tutored. Even when the expectation is friendship, the nondisabled peer should be at least as old as the peer with disabilities, and research indicates that a couple of years advantage for the nondisabled peer is even better.

■ Problem: Lack Of Preparation For Integration In New Situations

After you have organized your own integrated program—carefully preparing nondisabled participations in how to socialize effectively and instructing adult volunteers in what roles to take as facilitators—you will need to assure that the same steps occur in other community environments in which you wish to have them participate. So, if your local bowling alley, library, or parks program is not yet fully prepared for integrated activity, loaning them this handbook may be very useful.

■ Problem: Lack Of Individualization

Individualization is a familiar concept for persons who routinely work with individuals who have disabilities. Often, it comes naturally after a while because of the frequent need to adapt activities for persons who cannot perform them in the usual way. But, sometimes planners don't realize that peers without disabilities may also need to be introduced to integrated activities in an individualized fashion. For example, some nondisabled teenagers feel insecure in their own identities and so have difficulty extending themselves comfortably to anyone, including people with disabilities. Younger children are usually easiest to integrate successfully, followed by high school age people and adults. Middle school and junior high school students are a mixed lot—some are terrific while some are painfully out of their element and need to be introduced slowly and carefully to integrated programming.

Failure to consider personal preferences will undermine even the most noble and enthusiastic integration efforts.

■ Problem: Failure To Take Advantage of Choice-Making Opportunities

Integration into activities does not automatically guarantee enjoyment for people with disabilities. It is possible that, after working many months to achieve community integration, parents and service providers will be frustrated because some people with disabilities do not want to participate in these integrated community recreation and educational activities. Recreation and education preferences are extremely individual and failure to consider those personal preferences will undermine even the most noble and enthusiastic integration efforts. Fortunately, consideration of individual preferences can be accomplished by allowing people with disabilities to sample various preselected activities, and then to choose activities in which they wish to participate from those samples. Research has shown that when people with disabilities are allowed to choose the activities in which they wish to participate, they are more eager to learn the skills necessary to participate, they more readily generalize those skills to other settings, and they are more likely to continue to participate in those activities. (Fletcher, D.)

Emphasizing the safety of all participants as your first concern will reap benefits for everyone. . .

■ Problem: Sacrificing Participant Safety In The Name Of Integration

One elementary school recently experienced a boycott of classes as parents kept their nondisabled children at home out of fear for their safety. The concern revolved around the presence in the classroom of a child with disabilities who was abusive toward other children. While the school's commitment to the integration of this child was admirable, it was inappropriate to sacrifice the safety of the nondisabled students in implementing that ideal. It is prudent to remind ourselves occasionally that our society, while evaluating altruism, also has a litigious element in it. Emphasizing the safety of all participants as your first concern will reap benefits for everyone in this program.

■ Problem: Peers Assuming Adult Teaching Roles

Occasionally, a nondisabled peer assumes a skill teaching role that should be assumed by an adult. If using a tutorial role assignment, avoid having the peer without disabilities teach "heavy duty" skills. For example, a nondisabled peer should not be expected to teach a peer with a disability how to apply deodorant, put on undergarments, or brush teeth. These are tasks that are best left to parents.

The preceding information adapted from "Together Successfully" by Rynders, J.E., and Schleien, S.J. (1991).

4

Meeting, Greeting, and Interacting

The Basics of Welcoming

In this chapter, you will be offered techniques that will assist you in initiating interaction. The following sections represent topics with which many people may lack experience, and may consider barriers to positive human exchange. In order to feel confident to welcome all people, we will learn about:

- Attitudes
- Communication
- Interaction Techniques

Attitudes And You
The Most Important Topic!

Attitudes are the foundation compliance with the Americans with Disabilities Act (ADA). However, a law cannot mandate or change attitudes. That is up to you. This chapter will look at attitudes related to individuals with disabilities.

Exercise Time!

1. Does a person's attitude always show?

2. What is handicapism?

3. Do people with disabilities automatically understand and accept people with other types of disabilities than their own?

These are some interesting questions we will address in this segment.

First let's define an attitude. Attitudes are a way of responding (positive or negative) to a person, place, or thing. Attitudes are learned, not inherited. They consist of three parts: cognitive (how we think), effective (how we feel), and behavioral (how we actually act or behave). For example:

I once knew a parent of a teen with a disability. The parent was a vocal advocate for integrated services for individuals with disabilities, and thus evidenced a positive attitude. Her real beliefs or feelings were hidden. She would not allow her son to go to any public park program (even those designed for individuals with disabilities) because she was afraid he would not be accepted. She wanted him protected and was eventually accused of child abuse, because she limited his life options so significantly.

What we see is not always a true representation of attitudes. Attitudes can be disguised.

For most persons with disabilities, attitudes about themselves and others play a significant role in their lives. These attitudes make a difference—a big difference. WHY? Because negative attitudes often result in the denial of life options.

Handicapism: Prejudice, misunderstanding, fear, dislike, or disregard of individuals with disabilities. This is one of the most prevalent prejudices in today's society. Yes, you could have bypassed agism, sexism, racism, or ethnocentricity in today's politically correct world. However, it is unlikely that you survived without getting a touch of handicapism—even if you live with a disability yourself.

Let's examine some common negative attitudes, or handicapism.

Perceptions

People with disabilities are often regarded as:

Helpless—needing assistance with all life activities

Not capable

Childlike/Eternal children

Not valued

Diseased or contagious

Suspicious, criminal, or sexual deviants

Super Person—exceptionally courageous or capable, just for living

Not Responsible

Pitiful

Sad

Nonsexual

Holy or *uniquely blessed*

Untouchable

Less than Human

Better off with their own kind

Generalization of disabilities—totally disabled rather than having a specific limitation

Let's look candidly at some of the names and labels people with disabilities live with.

They include crippled, gimp, retard, spaz, vegetable, ortho, crazy, idiot, deaf and dumb, and the latest, Jerry's Kid. Even in our everyday language, we use disability terms to connote negativity. "What an idiot you are. Are you blind?

THE WAY WE ARE PERCEIVED AFFECTS THE WAY WE ARE TREATED.

Exercise Time!

Discuss the following questions:

1. How do you treat a person you perceive to be helpless?

2. How do you treat a person you believe to be competent and valuable?

Individuals with disabilities are faced with many negative attitudes that often result in behaviors that are evidence of handicapism. If one shows evidence of handicapism, he/she will reject, ignore, distance, exclude, overprotect, overhelp, devalue, deny access or choices to the disabled, and/or treat the disabled like children.

The way a person with a disability is treated may affect the way he/she acts.

Q: Have you ever returned home to your parents residence after being on your own, either to stay or for a visit? Did you act differently than you usually do? Why?

The way we are perceived affects the way we are treated.

And the way we are treated affects the way we act.

This is the self-fulfilling prophecy. It plays a big role in each person's life.

It holds special importance in the world of attitudes and individuals with disabilities.

If you perceive a person as incapable, then it is likely that you will treat him/her in a way that reinforces your belief. For example, an adult who has a visual impairment registers for a craft class. Because you feel he/she will not do well in the class, you might: (a) do things for him/her, or (b) not give him/her the instructions in a useful way. Your attitude says it's a lost cause. When the person who has a visual impairment receives this type of treatment, his/her response may be affected. He/she may have decreased belief in himself/herself, and expect to have excessive assistance in the future. This fulfills a circular loop. The way a person is perceived affects the way a person is treated and the way a person is treated affects that way a person acts.

This self-fulfilling prophecy can be used in a positive way! When people are asked to do something important because they are perceived as competent, they usually respond to the challenge. They give it their very best effort, and the results are usually good. Why? The way people are perceived affects the way people are treated, and the way people are treated affects the way people act. This point is very important in understanding and changing beliefs, ideas, feelings, treatments, and actions related to individuals with disabilities.

POSITIVE BELIEFS INSPIRE POSITIVE ACTIONS!

Exercise Time!

1. Please discuss and brainstorm: How do we change negative attitudes about individuals with disabilities?

The best way to change negative attitudes about individuals with disabilities is to get to know individuals with disabilities. Empathy, respect, understanding, and unconditional positive regard can be fostered quickly with a little rubbing of elbows.

Many different techniques can be used successfully to help a person get closer to individuals who have disabilities. Proximity and closeness are the best weapons against negative attitudes and prejudices.

2. How can we get closer to individuals who have disabilities?

Simulations

- Try using a wheelchair for at least three hours.

- Get up in the morning and get ready for your day without using your best hand or your eyes.

- Cover swim goggle lenses in a variety of ways (e.g., different shapes of paper, tape, petroleum jelly) to test different types of vision loss.

- Try the goggles and ear plugs, and have someone else try to instruct you in a simple, yet unknown task.

- Put noisy music on your headphones, your hand in a bucket of ice or wear clumsy gloves or mittens and try to play a complicated game you don't know well to simulate head injury or stroke.

- Do small group discussions about what you did over the weekend, with NO TALKING or writing allowed (explore the world of gesture and sign language).

Face-to-Face

- Visit programs or services that individuals with disabilities attend.

- Cross-train: all staff rotate to programs serving individuals with disabilities, not just the special recreation or therapeutic recreation team.

- Attend conferences, workshops and advocacy meetings sponsored by local disability related agencies and organizations.

- Invite guest speakers with disabilities to present at your agency.

- Volunteer to be a leisure buddy to a person with a disability.

- Attend events such as theater, art or sports programs that include or feature persons with disabilities.

- Spend some time, company picnic, softball game or camping trip with a peer or employee who has a disability.

Go to the Video Tapes

• Regular television series include persons with disabilities.

• Many popular big screen movies deal with issues related to disabilities. Catch them at the theater or wait until they come out on video.

• Many interesting films and videos are available to enhance understanding and attitudes related to individuals with disabilities. See Resources (page 145).

Watch Your Language!

Language reflects attitudes.

Individual or person with a disability is the current proper term to use. Use of an adjective as a noun such as *the disabled, the handicapped or the crippled* is OUT. Putting the adjective first, such as *the cerebral palsy boy* focuses too much on the disability and not the person. It should read: boy with cerebral palsy, or most of the time just: boy.

Using an adjective rather than a name is also OUT. *The blind kid . . .* is really Randy Smith. Using a little child's name rather than an adult name for an adult is OUT. If John is 20-years-old, then *he is not a Johnnie* unless his wife calls him that endearingly.

Individuals who use wheelchairs is the proper term. That is just what they are. They are not confined to a *wheelchair . . .* a wheelchair is a mobility device that frees consumers to go and do.

A person with or who has diabetes is proper terminology. Do not call someone who has diabetes a diabetic. A person does not become his/her disease. For example:

• instead of "diabetic" use "person with diabetes;"

• instead of "manic depressive" use "person with bipolar diseases;"

• instead of "amputee" use "individual who has an amputation;" or,

• instead of "hemophiliac" use "individual who has hemophilia."

To use *inflicted with* or *suffering from* is to put your poor attitude in the picture. These words or phrases that represent poor attitudes are often called CLANGERS (words that ring a bell of differentness). They consider the disability before the individual. They need to be avoided. Always use "person-first" terminology. Put the individual BEFORE the disability.

Adapted from: Dattilo, J. and Smith, R. W. (1990). "Community and Positive Attitudes Toward People With Disabilities Through Sensitive Terminology," *Therapeutic Recreation Journal, 24,* pp. 8-17.

Face-To-Face for the First Time? One Dozen Hints

A few hints on interacting with individuals with disabilities are provided below.

1. **You and the person with a disability are more alike than different.** All people have wishes, desires, hopes, and dreams. All people have things they can do and things they cannot do. The person with a disability is just like everyone else and wants to be seen and honored as a person first, having a disability second.

2. **Believe that you can communicate.** You may not be an expert but you can gesture, write a note, read body language, and even interpret different speech, if you try.

3. **Honor each person with unconditional positive regard (UPR).** This means that no matter who they are, you respect them and believe in their right to life and leisure. NO EXCEPTIONS.

4. **It's OK to ask most questions** regarding a person's disability in a polite manner. "It would be helpful for me to know what type of vision problems you have. Would you mind telling me what they are?" They will answer if they choose.

5. **Do not assume.** This means do not make up your mind about people in advance. What a person is like, what a person can do or not do, what a person likes or dislikes, and what his/her past experiences have been cannot be determined until you get to know them. Let them tell you, teach you, and show you.

6. **Do not generalize.** A rose is not a rose is not a rose. Each person will have a different degree, type, and response to a specific disability. No two persons who have had strokes are the same.

7. **Avoid being overprotective, overhelpful, or 'smother love.'** Avoid pity. Ask if they need or want help.

8. **Assist if there is a potential danger.** It is a professional judgement call for you to make.

9. **Be YOURSELF.** This means talking, laughing, and giving positive and negative feedback about behaviors and actions just as you would with anyone else.

10. **Use Humor!** Humor really helps dispel potentially uncomfortable feelings. If you are struggling to understand someone's speedy sign language, you might humorously put on your glasses and ask for repetition. In many instances, well intended humor helps break the tension felt by both parties.

11. **Expect the best of yourself,** yet know you can ask for assistance if you can't figure a situation out. Ask the consumer, your colleagues, an advocacy agency, parent, friend or any appropriate resource.

12. **Be prepared to change a bit**—get out of your usual mode of thinking, feeling, and operating. Knowing persons with disabilities will add to your life. It will alter your perspectives, beliefs, and values about yourself, people, and the community.

13. **Have Fun—That is what it is about.**

Communication

This segment is about total communication. It will help you become more confident in communicating with people who have a disability. The first section will inform you about general techniques. At the end of this section, a handout from the American Speech-Language-Hearing Association titled *Communication and the ADA* is provided (page 72).

Total communication simply means looking at communication in a much bigger and more flexible way than one might be used to. Total communication indicates the use of a wide variety of methods including speech, sign language, gestures, pictures, symbols, body language, writing, cues, and assistive devices to get the message across. We will explore these techniques briefly after we go over some basics of good communication.

Good communication skills start with understanding that communication is a process with several components.

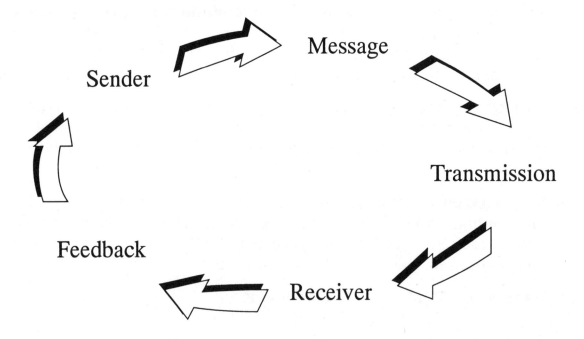

A humorous example of this communication loop: A supervisor at a fast food restaurant tells a worker who has deafness and autism to remove his belt pack (a cherished personal item) because it does not fit into the proper uniform regulations. Sender voices the message "take that off!" Transmission is via voice. Receiver does not hear or read lips.

He does not receive the message in his form of communication. A second attempt by the sender "Take that off, I told you!" No response. Sender now makes a lunge at the belt pack to physically remove it. Receiver gets a message. He strikes out at the supervisor with his message and feedback, stating in nonverbal language, "Keep your hands off my wallet!"

Communication is a process that needs to be carefully analyzed to insure that messages are understood. Two parts of good communication are: (1) understanding the message, and (2) communicating this understanding back to the sender.

Active listening is one key. First, assume eye level with the sender. That means sit or bend/squat slightly when speaking with a person who uses a wheelchair. Squarely face the person you are communicating with and make frequent eye contact. Lean forward a bit and have an open body position (not all crossed, folded and resistive looking).

Note the verbal (words), and expressed (tone), and nonverbal intent (body language) of the communication. Reflect what you believe is the intent of the message back to the sender to check if you are on target.

If you do not understand, DO NOT FAKE IT. Try it again and again. Try it in another mode. Ask for assistance. Finally, if you do not understand, state this.

Communication is a loop of sending and receiving messages, and getting feedback. The question to ask is: "Did I really understand?"

These basics of communication will assist you as you explore the use of some different kinds of communication that you may not be familiar with.

About Mode

Mode means the different ways people give and receive communication. The most common modes are auditory, visual and kinesthetic, or touch. The key is for the sender and receiver to be able to match the mode. The fast food supervisor in the previous example did not match his mode with the receiver. You can't speak French to a Japanese speaking person and expect good communication, unless both speak the same language.

Variety of Modes

Touch Communication. One of the most direct types of communication comes through touch. A light tap on the shoulder, high-five, handshake, or pat on the back are forms of touch communication. Avoid demeaning touch such as a pat on the head to an adult in a wheelchair. Always ask permission before touching a person. This can be done verbally (i.e., would you like a hug?) or physically (i.e., extending a hand for a handshake and waiting for the other person to reciprocate). Touching without permission is an invasion of personal boundaries.

DO With ME or Tactile Communication. Sometimes called coactive movement, this is one way to demonstrate a movement or activity to someone who may not be able to utilize visual or verbal communication well. You arrange for your consumer/learner to be in a position so that they can do what you are doing with you. They learn by feeling your motions as they move simultaneously with you.

Example: Teaching a person who has deaf-blindness or other major sensory deficits to cross-country ski, you as the leader, may allow the person to touch you to gain an understanding of your stance. A five seconds touch duration limit before disengaging is the current protocol to preclude illusions of sexual harassment of intimacy. The same technique could be used to teach a craft by placing the consumers hand lightly over yours as you lead the activity. They learn by doing and through the mode of touch. They disengage from you as they choose.

Gesture. Charades can be very helpful in getting across a message when language is not understood well. Facial gestures and using the whole body to mime or mimic an action or situation can often be understood well.

Imitation/Demonstration. "Do as I Do" communication is used for people who can learn by observing. An example: The tennis teacher demonstrates a stroke. The students imitate. Some people may have trouble with reversing the information on their body if the teacher is facing them. So teach a skill both facing the student and then facing away, so they get the front and back picture.

Verbal Imitation. When meeting a person with a unique speech pattern for the first time, it may be difficult to understand them. By matching the pacing, lip movement, and breath pattern of the person in a subtle type of copying, you may be able to grasp what they are saying better.

Symbols. These are visual, tactile, or olfactory (smell) signs that need to be decoded for understanding. One of the most common symbols in the world of disabilities is the international symbol of access.

An internationally recognized symbol system has been developed that would be used by individuals who have speech impairments and would bridge the gap between language differences. This symbol system is called the Bliss Symbol System.

Sign Language. This is language expressed with hand signals. Several types exist in the U.S. They are American Sign Language (ASL), SEE Sign, and the manual alphabet. ASL is the most commonly used. Individuals with hearing impairments and others that find it useful to express themselves via motion use sign language. It does not follow English grammar or syntax. SEE Sign is English on the hands, which is an adaptation of ASL that more formally follows English language formats. The manual alphabet or fingerspelling is included in both of the above and is basically a way of spelling using sign.

Fingerspelling Alphabet

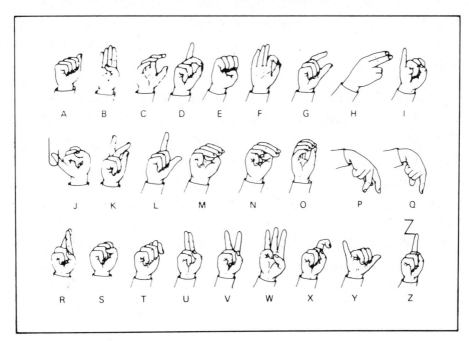

Tadoma, or Touch Signing is a means by which a person who has a vision and hearing impairment feels sign language. It is signing in the hand.

Scanning. This is a technique that is used in many different ways. It is the review of various choices or options so that the consumer can select the desired message. Verbal scanning is when a person is offered a variety of options (for various reasons either they can't see the option or have limited verbal expression). Example: "What would you like for lunch, John? We have hamburgers . . . (wait for response) . . . hot dogs . . . (wait) . . . salads. John's response may be a head nod, finger tap, smile or verbal "OK." Each person's response system will have to be determined individually, usually by some type of yes or no signal.

Communication Devices. Scanning may be done with the assistance of an augmentative communication device. These include communication boards where a person scans options and points or selects messages. The options may be a picture or symbol, one word, short phrases, or built into longer sentences. Your job is to do reflective listening and to make sure the correct message is being interpreted.

Communication boards have gone techno. Many types of communication boards now use computers and scan electronically. Selections are made using a toggle switch, input into a computer, and digitally printed out. Some even have a voice synthesizer unit to simulate speech. These come in all sizes and shapes, from hand held pocket units to larger nonportable styles.

Other Devices and Options. People with throat dysfunctions may use a hand-held vibrating unit to allow speech. It does sound very nasal, but it works. Individuals who have visual and hearing impairments have a difficult time getting attention, when needed, because they have no way of knowing who is around them. If they are crossing a street, they may use a taped message machine which speaks, "Please assist me, I am deaf and blind." Talking books, calculators, and computers are now available for those who would like to use a verbal message. Technology has also created machines that can read printed materials aloud.

TDD. The Telephone Device for the Deaf (TDD) is basically a form of digital-type communication. One person types over the phone lines to another TDD receiver. If you do not have a TDD to give or receive a message, then a relay service can be used. With the ADA these are no longer a luxury, but a necessity for human service agencies.

Relay Service. Your local phone company has a relay service, free of extra charge. If you are a voice user and do not have a TDD, send your message through the relay service. If you are not able to use voice, you TDD your message to the relay and they interpret it to the hearing person.

Dogs And Other Animal Assistants. Yes, dogs are learning sign language! Well in actuality, they are being trained to signal. For example, a person who is deaf cannot hear a fire alarm, the working companion dog is trained to call attention to the problem.

As you can see there are many different modes of communication and using the correct mode is the first step in sending a message that can be received.

Exercise Time!

Discuss the following questions:

1. What if you do not know the best mode of the receiver you intend to send a message to?

2. What if you have a group of people who have various types of modes?

Answer:

Use Total Communication! Your Voice, Gestures, Demonstrations, Illustrations, Examples, Signals, Symbols, Written Information, Sign Language, Observation, And Your Creativity.

Timing

1. **Be sure the person is ready for your message.** Get their attention. Observe to see if they are positioned and ready to receive your message.

2. **Eliminate distractions.** Giving important instructions to a distractible group of kids while a cute dog wanders around is poor timing.

3. **Allow more time.** Deciphering messages, interpreting, scanning and word finding may take at least twice as long if not longer.

4. **Do not interrupt, fill-in, or speak for a person with slow speech.** Wait for them to finish.

Tuning In

Since more than 60 percent of our communication is nonverbal, use your skills of observation. When someone is communicating to you, ASK yourself the question, *"What are they really trying to tell me?"* That they are shy? confident? bored? excited? nervous or unsure? delighted? being flirtatious? or *at leisure*?

When you are communicating a message, ASK, "Did they really understand? There is a "yes, I understand" signal within us all. It usually is in the eyes, that glint of understanding when the light bulb goes on. If a person doesn't use their eyes to tell you this, then perhaps it is in the subtlest gesture, head nod, or eye blink. If you cannot get confirmation of understanding in this way, do a real life check: a test of information based on real actions and outcomes.

Helpful Hints About Communication

1. **Speak to the person**, not the interpreter, parent, counselor or attendant!

2. **Be honest.**

3. **Be confident you can do it**. Fear of initiations is the main barrier for most people. You do not have to be an expert.

4. **Do not fake it**.

5. **Allow for more time**.

6. **Use total communication and multimodal techniques.**

7. **Get on the right wave length: Mode, Timing and Tuning.**

8. **Be observant.**

9. **Get feedback, and perception check**. "Did I really understand? Was I really understood?"

10. **Be yourself.**

11. **Humor can work wonders!**

COMMUNICATION

"We Have Ways"

WAYS
- Touch
- Coactive Movement
- Gesture
- Body language
- Tadoma/Scanning
- Reverse imitation/Direct mirror imitation
- Demonstration

FACTORS
- MODE
- TIMING
- TUNING
- HONESTY

SYMBOLS
- BLISS symbols
- Braille
- Word boards
- Sign language
- Finger spelling
- Electronic aided devices
- Computer voice synthesizers

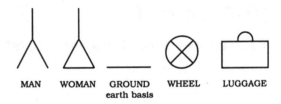

MAN   WOMAN   GROUND earth basis   WHEEL   LUGGAGE

Examples of BLISS symbols

The following document, Communication and the ADA (found on pages 73-80), is available in the following formats: large print, audiotape, computer disk, braille, electronic bulletin board (202-514-6193).

This document provides general information to promote voluntary compliance with the Americans with Disabilities Act (ADA). It was prepared under a grant from the U.S. Department of Justice. While the Office on the Americans with Disabilities Act has reviewed its contents, any opinions or interpretations in the document are those of the American Speech-Language-Hearing Association and do not necessarily reflect the views of the Department of Justice. The ADA itself and the Department's ADA regulations should be consulted for further, more specific guidance.

Produced by American Speech-Language-Hearing Association, 10801 Rockville Pike, Rockville, MD 20852, 1-800-638-8255 (V/TDD), 301-897-5700 (V); 301-897-0157 (TDD).

Communication and the ADA
(Effective Communication and Accessibility)

**What is
EFFECTIVE
COMMUNICATION
under ADA?**

- **Taking steps to ensure** that people with communication disabilities:

    - Have **access to goods, services, and facilities**

    - Are **not excluded, denied services, seg-regated or otherwise treated differently** than other people

- **Making information accessible to and usable by** people with communication disabilities

**What is required
to achieve
EFFECTIVE
COMMUNICATION
under ADA?**

- **Providing any necessary auxiliary communication aids and services:**

    - Unless an undue burden or a fundamental change in the nature of the goods, services, facilities, etc. would result

    - Without a surcharge to the individual

- **Making aurally (via hearing) delivered information available** to persons with hearing and speech impairments (including alarms, nonverbal speech, and computer-generated speech):

- Personally prescribed devices such as hearing aids are **not** required.

How do you determine NECESSARY AUXILIARY COMMUNICATION AIDS AND SERVICES?

- Consideration of:

  - **Expressed preference of the individual with disability.**

  - **Level and type of the communication exchange** (complexity, length, and importance of material). For example, interpreter services might not be necessary for a simple business transaction such as buying groceries, but they might be appropriate in lengthy or major transactions such as purchasing a car or provision of legal or medical services.

- **Selection of appropriate aids and services** from available technologies and services (low-tech as well as high-tech) based on facility resources and communication needs (individual's and type of material).

What are STRATEGIES for achieving EFFECTIVE COMMUNICATION?

- **Establishing appropriate attitudes and behaviors:**

  - Assuming that persons with communication disabilities can express themselves if afforded the opportunity, respect, and the necessary assistance to do so

  - Consulting the person with the disability how best to communicate with him or her, and asking about the need for aids and services

  - Training staff to communicate more effectively

- **Modifying the communication setting,** for example, reducing noise levels. Improving the communication setting can also reduce the need for assistive devices in some cases.

What are STRATEGIES for achieving EFFECTIVE COMMUNICATION?
(continued)

- **Providing auxiliary aids and services**

- **Responding to auxiliary aids and services requests**

- **Providing materials in accessible formats** (e.g., written transcripts)

- **Keeping written materials simple and direct**

- **Providing visual as well as auditory information**

- **Providing a means for written exchange of information**

- **Informing public of available accommodations**

- **Maintaining devices in good working condition**

- **Consulting a professional** (audiologist, speech-language pathologist)

What are examples of COMMUNICATION (SPEECH AND HEARING) AIDS AND SERVICES?

- **In assembly areas, meetings, and conversations:**

  - Assistive listening devices and systems (ALDs), communication boards (word, symbol), qualified interpreters (oral, cued speech, sign language), real-time captioning, written communication exchange and transcripts, computer-assisted note taking, lighting on speaker's face, preferential seating for good listening and viewing position, electrical outlet near accessible seating, videotext displays

What are examples of COMMUNICATION (SPEECH AND HEARING) AIDS AND SERVICES?
(continued)

- **In telecommunications:**

  - Hearing aid compatible telephones, volume control telephone handsets, amplified telephone mouthpieces (for person with weak voice) (to amplify speech for a hard-of-hearing listener), telecommunication device for the deaf (TDD) or text telephone, facsimile machines (that use visual symbols), computer/modem, interactive computer software with videotext

  - TDD/telephone relay systems

- **In buildings:**

  - Alerting, signaling, warning, and announcement systems using amplified auditory signals, visual signals (flashing, strobe), vibrotactile (touch) devices, videotext displays

- **In prepared (nonlive) materials:**

  - Written materials in alternate formats (e.g., symbols, pictures)

  - Aurally-delivered materials in alternate formats (e.g., captioned videotapes, written transcript, sign interpreter)

  - Notification of accessibility options (e.g., alternative formats)

What are COMMUNICATION BARRIERS?

- Factors that hinder or prevent information coming to and/or from a person

- **Visually-related barriers**

  - Inadequate or poor lighting/poor background that interferes with ability to speechread or see signing

What are COMMUNICATION BARRIERS?
(continued)

- Unreadable signage (too small, not in line of vision of people in wheelchairs or of short stature)

- Lack of visual information (e.g., not showing speaker's face)

- Lack of signage and accessibility symbols

• **Acoustically-related barriers**

- High noise levels

- High reverberation levels

- Lack of aurally-delivered information to supplement visual information (for example, not using amplified auditory as well as visual signals in emergency alarms, partitions that block sound between speaker and listener)

• **Attitudinal and prejudicial barriers**

• **Information complexity** (such as difficult reading level)

What is required for COMMUNICATION ACCESSIBILITY under ADA?

• **Providing TDD and accessible telephone or alternative service**

- When telephone service is regularly provided to customers/patients on more than just an incidental basis (e.g., hospitals, hotels)

- When building entry requires aural or voice information exchange (e.g., closed circuit security telephone)

• **Providing means for two-way communication in emergency situations** (e.g., elevator emergency notification system) that does not require hearing or speech for communication exchange

**What is
required for
COMMUNICATION
ACCESSIBILITY
under ADA?**
(continued)

- **Providing closed caption decoders,** upon request, in hospitals that provide televisions, and in places of lodging with televisions in five or more guest rooms

- **Removing structural communication barriers** in existing buildings when readily achievable (inexpensively and easily removed)

- **Providing alternative service** when barriers are not easily removed (e.g., preferential seating area)

- **Following accessibility standards** for new construction/alterations (ADA Accessibility Guidelines, Uniform Federal Accessibility Standard)

**What are some
READILY
ACHIEVABLE
STRUCTURAL
BARRIER
REMOVAL
STRATEGIES?**

- **Installing sound buffers** to reduce noise and reverberation

- **Installing flashing alarm lights** in restrooms, any general usage areas, hallways, lobbies, and any other common usage areas

- **Integrating visual alarms** into facility alarm systems

- **Removing physical partitions** that block sound or visual information between employees and customers

- **Providing directional signage** with symbols to indicate available services

What is needed for signage and symbols of communication accessibility?

- **Symbols** for:

  - **Telephone** accessibility:

    - blue grommet between cord and handset—"hearing aid compatible"

    - telephone handset with radiating soundwaves—"volume control"

  - **TDDs** or text telephones—the international TDD symbol

- **Signage:**

  - **Directional signage** indicating nearest TDD or accessible telephone

  - **Messages for availability of Assistive Listening Devices** (ALDs) in announcements, in key building areas

  - **Messages for communication aids and services** (e.g., interpreters)

International Symbol of Accessibility

International TDD Symbol

Telephone Handset Amplification Symbol

What types of POLICIES AND PRACTICES NEED TO BE MODIFIED?

- Discriminatory policies such as prohibiting hearing assistance dogs

- Discriminatory eligibility criteria such as restricting access to goods and services unless necessary for the provision of goods and services

What is the best way to ensure COST-EFFECTIVE ADA COMPLIANCE?

- **Perform a facility accessibility audit** that includes identification of communication barriers

- **Determine auxiliary aids and services needs**

- **Develop a plan to remove barriers and acquire assistive devices**

- **Perform ongoing audit and maintenance of accessibility features**

- **Modify discriminatory policies, practices, and procedures**

- **Obtain technical assistance and consult** with rehabilitation professionals, disability organizations, consumers, federal agencies as appropriate

The BOTTOM LINE

- Ask people about their needs, show respect and sensitivity, use what works (not necessarily what is most expensive), use your resources creatively and effectively.

Interaction Techniques

This section will address some generic skills of interaction that may or may not be familiar. They are relevant to various aspects of some of the most common disabilities. We will look at:

- Working and playing with individuals with learning differences

- Wheelchairs and devices (and the people who use them)

- Basic transfer training

- Inappropriate behaviors

- Seizures: What to do

Working And Playing With Individuals With Learning Differences

These hints apply in a general way to many different people who have a learning style difference.

1. Before beginning an activity, review safety rules and special needs with consumers.

2. When presenting instructions use multimodal communication. Use concrete, direct, and short sentences. Provide one part of the instruction at a time rather than a 10-minute speech.

3. Demonstration and *"Do as I Do"* learning is very useful.

4. Break the activity down into small sequential steps. Teach each step progressively, noting and adjusting to the speed of the learner.

5. Allow plenty of time for learning and relearning.

6. Attention spans may be short, so allow for breaks or alternative activities during a long task.

7. Noncompetitive activities allow for inclusion of individuals with varied skill levels.

8. See Program Adaptations (page 97) for more inclusion ideas.

9. Emphasize choice, age appropriateness, and independence. Encourage consumers to make their own choices, and do for themselves what they can.

10. Communication styles may differ. See Communication (page 64).

11. Appropriate reinforcement assists in building confidence and skills. Do not provide unwarranted or false praise.

12. Expectations play a major role in our leadership style. THINK POSITIVE!

Wheelchairs and Devices

Individuals with disabilities often use assistive devices. These include everything from glasses and hearing aids, to computerized voice synthesizers and respirators.

Common devices you may encounter may cause you concern if you do not know what they are or how to use them. Here are some basics.

The device is valuable to the person and often is life and freedom giving. Do not underestimate its importance by mistreating it. If you do not know what to do, ASK.

Wheelchair: A rolling chair. Remember, the term is not 'confined to' but a 'person who uses a wheelchair.' There are many varieties of wheelchairs. Manual (self-push), Power (motorized), Sports (modified for speed and maneuverability), All-Terrain (like a little tank), and Scooter-chairs (bigger and often three-wheeled). Some people who use wheelchairs can stand and walk to some degree, yet choose to use a chair for speed, convenience or appearance.

Gurney: A rolling bed.

Crutches: A device (or devices) that provides mobility support from under the arm or upper arm to ground. There are regular wooden ones, or metal ones, and ones with cuffs on them. Some are used individually; some are used in pairs.

Canes: A device, grasped in the hand, that is used for mobility support. There are straight ones, three-footed ones, folding ones, and fancy ones.

Walkers: A device that provides mobility support that looks something like a movable gate. Many styles include wheels, and some are collapsible.

Prosthesis: An artificial limb such as a leg, foot or arm. Some are cosmetic, many are functional.

Ileostomy and Colostomy Bags: These are devices that collect body waste (fecal material) and replace natural elimination functions.

Catheter: Any device that shuttles materials, usually liquids, from one place to another. A urine catheter is often used by a person with quadriplegia. You may notice some people have a portable catheter on their wheelchair or leg. Often they are hidden from sight.

Respirators: Devices that regulate and assist breathing. Portable units are often carried in packs or placed under wheelchairs.

Voice Synthesizers: An electronic word board that speaks.

Communication Boards: A board with lists of words, phrases, pictures or symbols to assist in communication. This may be used via pointing, or electronic scanning. See Communication (page 64).

Head Sticks: A pointer stick on a head band to allow a person who does not use their hands to point, type or play checkers.

Joy Stick: The toggle switch of an electric wheelchair that controls its speed and direction.

A zillion other assistive devices exist.

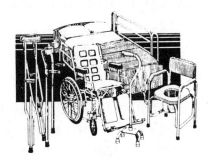

What To Do With Wheelchairs

(and the people who use them!)

The Basics

1. Know that the wheelchair is valuable. Treat the chair like a precious object.

2. Wheelchairs do roll. They have locks that need to be in place over each wheel when a person desires to be stationary.

If Consumers Are Going Somewhere . . .

3. Do not assume a person in a chair needs to be pushed.

4. Ask before you do anything, "What would be the best way for me to assist you?"

5. Before pushing a person who is using a wheelchair, check to see if a person's feet are on the foot rests, not on the floor or tangled up underneath. Check to see if hands, fingers, or catheters might be near or in the wheels. Check the breaks and the safety belt or other positioning equipment that may need to be strapped or fastened.

6. Most people in wheelchairs prefer to face the direction they are traveling. This helps solve the questions you may have about which way to go up or down a curb. The answer is *Forward* most of the time.

7. Wheelchairs have big back wheels, little front rollers, and a tipping lever in the back. When you go up a curb, you tip the chair back so the little wheels go up on the curb first.

8. When going down a curb, tip the chair back (a wheelie) and lower the chair on it's big back wheels evenly. If a person is heavy, you may want to go down a curb backwards. ASK FIRST.

9. NEVER CARRY A PERSON UP OR DOWN STAIRS IN A WHEELCHAIR. Unless there is an emergency, this is demeaning and is not true accommodation. In some rugged outdoor terrain, carrying the person and the chair may be OK. Ask the person how he/she feels about this first.

10. Never take a wheelchair away from a person without asking. Inform him/her why you think you need to remove it (safety hazard). Always try to place the wheelchair within the person's reach, or nearby and be sure he/she knows where it is in case of emergency.

11. Folding a wheelchair—ASK. Most fold up by pulling up on the seat. Arms of most chairs, as well as foot rests, are removable. Newer models are equipped with quick release levels to remove the wheels.

12. Storing chairs takes space. Use a car trunk for one, or an extra truck for several chairs on a trip.

13. When assisting a person using a wheelchair onto a van lift, be sure to secure any wheel locks and the roll preventing gates on the lift.

14. Check the van out for safety belts. Yes, they have them—probably several of them—one for the person, and one for the chair. USE THEM!

15. If you need to assist in the transfer of a person from a wheelchair to a car seat, couch, poolside, etc., you will want to consider getting training in what is known as "transfers."

Basic Transfer Training

1. Your back is very important to you. If you want to keep it injury-free, do not rely on it for lifting or carrying anything!

2. Use your leg and buttock muscles to lift; these are your strong muscles.

3. Practice a ballet plié. Stand, plié, stand. Do not bend over from the waist. Keep your torso upright as you squat down and stand up. This is the move you will use to assist a person from chair to chair, or whatever.

4. GET READY! Wheelchair locked in place. Surface to transfer to secure. PLEASE! No sliding away targets!

5. Take off the arm of the wheelchair that will be in the way. Most are removable. Remove or flip up foot rests.

6. Get the chair and surface you are going to close. Place/arrange at a 45° angle on the most functional side of the person so they can help.

7. Discuss the move with your consumer. Develop a plan for the move. A count like "One, Two, Three, GO!" may be useful.

8. Consumers are not a sack of potatoes. Use their strengths and ask for their complete cooperation.

9. Have the person scoot to the edge of the wheelchair or assist them in doing so.

10. Position their feet firmly on the floor (parallel with feet flat on the ground) with knees bent.

11. If possible have them grasp around your torso or upper arms. NOT YOUR NECK.

12. You grasp around their mid- to lower back or use a transfer belt (which can be purchased at a medical supply company), not under the arms and avoiding chest/breasts.

13. Push your knees up against theirs to stabilize them.

14. Do the count, lift, pivot with a straight back and gently lower the person into the other chair.

15. You may often need the assistance of another person to lift the consumer. WHEN IN DOUBT, ASK FOR ASSISTANCE!

16. Assist the person in rearranging themselves in the chair, seat, wheelchair, etc.

17. If possible, ask a nurse or physical therapist to train your staff to transfer individuals who use wheelchairs.

Checklist For Basic Transfers
(wheelchair to chair)

Discuss and Plan

Think SAFETY First, YOURS AND THE CONSUMERS

Seek assistance if needed

Get Your Environment Situated

GET READY!

Consumer Scoot to Edge

Place Feet

Brace Knees

Plié Down

Grasp around back

Do the Count

Stand-Lift (Plié Up)

Pivot

Plié Down

Assist/Readjust

Exercise Time!

Practicing this technique is very useful, (no, not on consumers) but with yourselves. In pairs, try doing transfers with each other. Give feedback to each other about how it felt—safe, unsafe, and how to improve. Use regular chairs if wheelchairs are not available.

Each transfer situation and each person will require a unique approach. Think safety first—yours and the participants'.

Inappropriate Behaviors

Inappropriate behavior is a term used to describe behavior that does not fit within a defined (often fairly vague) standard or norm. The same behavior can be viewed as appropriate or inappropriate depending on the role of the person doing the behavior, the timing of the behavior, or the situation in which the behavior is acted out. The following are very basic suggestions on how to deal with behaviors deemed inappropriate in a recreation setting. Teaching behavior modification, a specific type of psychological treatment, is NOT the intent.

1. Allow for individual differences in behavior that are not disruptive or harmful. Does it really matter if the kid with autism is spinning and laughing for a few minutes? Ask yourself if the consequences of the behavior are really negative to the person or program before you label them inappropriate.

   Consumers must be encouraged to explore who they are and to be themselves in their leisure. Recreation leaders need to accept them for whom they are. Consequently, behaviors and situations must be weighed very carefully before placing a judgment and label on a consumer's behavior.

2. Concentrate on the behavior you would like to see. Clearly state, model, and demonstrate this behavior.

3. Reward attempts, even partial attempts, of the desired behavior.

4. Provide visible models of good behavior.

5. Provide clear instructions, regulations, rules of conduct and precautions. Let the consumers help develop or refine 'rules'.

6. Redirect actions. Take a walk, change the conversation, start a new activity or twist to the game.

7. Define the consequences of inappropriate or unacceptable behavior. Make sure the person understands the potential results of continued inappropriate behavior.

8. If inappropriate behavior continues, give a verbal and confidential warning . . . "If this continues, you will have to sit out for five minutes," or if extreme, "This is your third warning, you will have to leave."

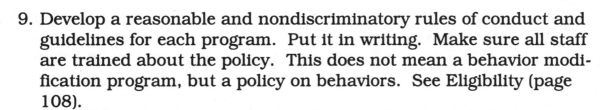

9. Develop a reasonable and nondiscriminatory rules of conduct and guidelines for each program. Put it in writing. Make sure all staff are trained about the policy. This does not mean a behavior modification program, but a policy on behaviors. See Eligibility (page 108).

10. Administer this policy with fair-handedness with all consumers, not just ones you have identified as trouble makers or having emotional problems.

11. Consider additional staffing. Some individuals with disabilities will need additional coaching in order to learn and maintain appropriate behaviors in a recreation setting.

12. Seek outside help from mental health professionals, teachers, or other appropriate staff or consultants if problems persist. The ADA requires various approaches to accommodation before exclusion from programs or services.

Seizures: What To Do

1. Do not try to control the person or stop the seizure.

2. Think safety. Assist the person to the ground, push any furniture or objects away. If they are in water or on a nonstable surface, get them to a stable surface as soon as possible. In water, a person should be supported in the water with the head tilted so his/her face and head stay above the surface. Once on a level surface, if the person is not breathing, artificial respiration should begin at once.

3. Loosen tight clothing around the neck. If needed, pop the button, as they may be struggling and you may not be able to grasp the button to undo it properly.

4. Do not put anything in the person's mouth. NOTHING, not a ruler, not your fingers, not a drink of water. NOTHING.

5. Cushion the head while not restraining it.

6. Turn head to the side to allow saliva to flow out and prevent choking. A person may have a tongue guard (a plastic device that prevents the person from biting their tongue). It goes in something like false teeth. Use it.

7. If a person is choking, a chin jut is useful. This is simply tipping the person's head back as they lie on their back, and inserting your thumbs under their jaw bones and pushing forward. This gets the persons head back and chin forward. This will help with swallowing when they are unconscious.

   This training comes with basic first aid which most recreation professionals have. GET A COURSE ON FIRST AID!

8. It may not be necessary to call for medical help or an ambulance unless:

   (a)   the seizure lasts for more than 5 minutes,

   (b)   if there is a series of serious seizures,

   (c)   if the person is pregnant, injured, or diabetic,

   (d)   if the seizure has happened in water,

   (e)   if there is no medical I.D. and no way of knowing whether the seizure is caused by epilepsy, or

   (f)   if consciousness does not return after the shaking has stopped.

   From: *Seizure Recognition and First Aid*, Epilepsy Foundation of America.

   These events are just part of life for the person, and unless they are prolonged, are not life threatening.

9. Get the other people, except for one assistant, away. People are naturally curious and curiosity is not needed at this time.

10. When the person regains consciousness, gently say something to the effect, "welcome back, I know you had a seizure and I am here to help. We will just rest here for a minute and then you can let me know what we do next."

11. Do not leave the person who has had a seizure. Stay with him/her for reassurance and to meet needs. He/she may insist on jumping right back into the activity, but may need to rest or even go home. He/she is often confused for a period of time and cannot usually travel without an escort.

When the person does return to the group, assist the other members in disability awareness through casual discussion. Dispel myths with the person's permission and carry on with the activity. If you note any type of negativity by others, take them aside and confront them on these issues. Invite them to a first-aid training on seizures, as it is usually fear of not knowing that keeps them in their handicapism worlds.

5

Program Planning

This chapter explores elements of program planning that need to be considered when addressing accommodation and inclusion of individuals with disabilities. The topics are:

- Activity Selection

- Activity Analysis

- Activity Modifications and Program Adaptation

- Public Relations

- ADA and Risk Management Plans

The purpose of this section is to provide strategies for planning programs that are truly accessible to individuals with disabilities. Four concepts will be discussed: Activity Selection, Activity Analysis, and Activity Modification and Program Adaptation.

Activity Selection

Exercise Time!

Discuss the following questions:

1. What is the main programming consideration in providing recreation activities for individuals with disabilities?

> *Answer: A person's choice is the first consideration in activity selection. The purpose of regular recreation is to fulfill leisure needs and desires.*
>
> *An individual's choices, rights, and desires are honored. The right to risk, and yes, even to fail, are human rights.*
>
> *A person with a disability may have limited experiences, limited memory, or limited ability to express true choices.*

2. An adult is asked, "What would you like to do for recreation?" He/she chooses, "Play on the swings." What would you do?

Activity selection processes include: scanning choices (See Communication, page 64), looking at pictures, and actual testing of a variety of activities. This question can be answered in many ways. The key to appropriate activity selection is helping the person identify his/her current choices. A person's leisure need not be limited by his/her past experiences.

Activity Analysis

This process focuses on identifying what it takes to complete an activity. This is a key skill for the leisure professional.

Exercise Time!

Divide into groups of two: One person takes off his/her shoe. This person is to act as if they do not know what a shoe is or how to put it on. The second person (coach) is to verbally direct the first person in putting the shoe on. Included in coaching is the role of motivator and cheer-leader. See how many steps it takes to complete the "simple" task of putting on a shoe.

Activity analysis is the process of identifying all the steps it takes to be able to participate in an activity. Next, an assessment of the consumer's skills can be completed and compared to the skills identified as necessary by the activity analysis. From there the gaps can be filled with strategies of modification, adaptation, coaching, and leisure education.

Example: The first step in participating in an exercise class at a gym might be to locate the entrance door of the gym from the bus drop off point. Initially, the person with a visual impairment may not be able to do this. With one or two times of assisted entry, they might be capable of doing this on their own.

Perhaps another step for exercise class participation is dressing. A person with multiple disabilities who uses a wheelchair may have to spend two hours dressing with the assistance of a personal aide. Yes, they could come early and do it at the gym, or perhaps an adaptation of dressing at home could be made.

Activity requirement may be to be able to engage in an aerobic routine for 20 minutes. The person with limited stamina may only be able to go for 10 minutes in the beginning. Activity requirement may be social graces in class (i.e, not talking when the instructor is talking). When a consumer who has a tendency to talk out loud is in class, he/

she may need a leisure buddy who will provide one-to-one coaching on social skills. Other participants and the leader can be cued to provide polite but needed feedback to the consumer.

Activity analysis and modification go hand in hand.

Activity analysis includes looking at the cognitive (thinking), affective (feeling and emotional) and physical (psychomotor, strength, stamina, and flexibility) requirements of an activity.

Exercise Time!

This exercise may be completed in small groups or individually. Analyze the level of skill needed to play golf. (1) Consider cognitive, affective and physical requirements. (2) Rank the importance of each of the three areas (cognitive, affective, and physical) on a scale of 1 to 5 with 1 being low, and 5 being high. You will find many different opinions on the importance of each area.

Of course, the context of the activity is important. A competition golf game versus a fun game of golf are two different situations, each having a different set of cognitive, affective, and physical requirements. Ask yourself:

What are the requirements of the activity related to?

Travel

Safety Skills

Communication

Rules

Environment

Personal Needs:
bathroom, eating, snacks during the program

Social Skills

Affective Skills

Cognitive Skills

Physical Skills

Leadership and Administrative Needs

Feasibility:
time, money, etc.

Ask: What does a person have to know, do, or feel to be able to be successful at this program or event? What skills, knowledge, or experience might the person be missing? This is where adaptation comes in.

Activity Modifications and Program Adaptation

Adaptations and modifications can be viewed from many perspectives. They may be environmental changes, such as requesting a portable, accessible restroom for a picnic. They may be changes in the activity itself, such as changing rules, staff, or equipment. They may be changes in the requirements themselves, such as allowing a person a two minute head start in a marathon.

Sometimes an activity analysis identifies huge differences between the requirements for an activity and the consumer's abilities. Then it is appropriate to think about adding an appropriate preactivity, lead up, or, on rare occasions, substitution or deletion of the activity.

The real challenge, fun, and success comes when activities are adjusted so well to the abilities of the individual participants that a true leisure experience results for all involved!

Exercise Time!

Do an activity analysis for each activity in column A. Then proceed to decide what modifications, adaptations or substitutions might be needed for an individual with the corresponding functional limitation from column B.

Let's practice some activity analysis and modifications.

A. *Activity Column*

1. Intricate folk dance routine
2. Egg (raw) rolling contest
3. Leading part in the theater play

B. *Functional Limitation*

1. Hearing impairment
2. Motor control impairment
3. Speech impairment

Program Adaptations

Exercise Time!

Discuss the following questions:

1. Does a person with a disability automatically need program adaptations?

2. Is expensive adaptive equipment always necessary for program adaptations.

Program adaptation is an important skill for the leisure professional. He/she must analyze a recreation activity, compare the requirements to participant's capabilities, and suggest adaptations if necessary. The goal is to make participation possible and equally rewarding for all participants.

Rules for Successful Program Adaptations

1. Adapt only if necessary.

2. Keep the format of the experience as close to normal as possible.

3. Ask the participant for input on what he/she needs and how to adapt the activity. Tailor the modification to the individual rather than the group.

4. Be creative! Believe that old ways are not always the best.

5. Think types of programming that focus on fun and participation rather than elimination like win, win, and new games.

6. Be realistic about the goal of the activity and its requirements. Is it necessary to see the target to play darts? No, it is not. The need is to identify where the target is and better yet, where the bull's-eye is.

7. If participants ask about an adaptation, be prepared to respond briefly with the rationale of the adaptations you make for a consumer with a disability.

Check Your Box!

Contributing Author: Ms. Terry Murray

If a person is perceived as unable to participate in an activity, he/she is put in the "Can't Do" box. Often this is due to inadequate accommodations for the person with a disability rather than an actual limitation. Change the situation to one that says, "Let's see what we can do!"

Goal of Activity

By definition expectation means to look forward to something. While developing a program, recreation leaders look forward to certain outcomes or successes. When including individuals with disabilities in recreation programs, the final outcome may, at times, be different from preconceived expectations. The participant's own success may be defined differently from the picture leaders have in their minds. To merge expectations with the participant's, ask these questions: (1) What is the ultimate goal of the activity? (2) What is the definition of successful participation? Ask those same questions of the participant with a disability. Compare answers and make the necessary accommodations to facilitate success.

Promote Inclusion And Success!

After attitudes and expectations are reviewed and shifted, activities are modified to promote inclusion and success. In the following section, a variety of modification procedures are explored. Remember to use creativity, and not to BOX in your thinking.

Change Rules

Although the basics of an activity should be retained as much as possible, rules can be changed to equalize competition. Instead of keeping score, an activity may be played for a specific amount of time. The number of points needed to conclude a game may be reduced or increased. A unique handicap system, used in such sports as golfing, where the scores are modified according to the players' average scores, or horse racing, where the "better" athletes must carry extra weight, can be established individually for each player or team. For example: A team might begin play with a predetermined number of points or allow a slower runner additional time or a head start.

Change Team or Group Formation

If the goal is more participation, subtract players from a group or team. If a large area needs to be covered, assign two or more people to each spot. Allow positions to be rotated frequently. Analyze the players' abilities and assign positions accordingly, but do not develop an 'on the bench' system. Tandem or buddy systems may be substituted for activities that are traditionally done individually with wonderful results in many instances.

Adjust Energy Requirements

Time of participation may be the variable that needs to be adjusted. The total length of playing time may be shortened. Free substitution allows a person to rest at their own discretion. Alternate vigorous and quiet type activities.

Adapt Space

The space needed for an activity may also be changed. Those with limited mobility, might benefit from a reduced size of the playing area. Indoors versus outdoors, a backstop instead of field, and a fenced in area are all adaptations that may allow for participation. Grass may slow down a ball, as well as a wheelchair. Blacktop with a reduced total area may be an alternative place to play baseball.

Change Skill Requirements

Dribbling a basketball while propelling a wheelchair is a difficult task. So, being allowed to travel is an alternative. How about putting everyone in wheelchairs to play on a more equitable level? A person with severe motor function problems may be allowed to talk or coach another through an activity as their 'player.' A slower player may be allowed additional time or a head start.

Change Equipment

A wider bat has helped many people learn baseball skills. A broad range of adaptive equipment is available. A rubber ball at the end of a paint brush allows for easier grasp. A light sensitive target beeps when the laser beam of the gun aims accurately at the target. This system can be used to allow a person with a visual impairment to participant in target shooting.

Juggle the rest,
only if needed...

...but hang on to the goal
of the activity!

Exercise Time!

In small groups or individually, take the following equipment, and create a game for kids: a pile of newsprint, and a roll of masking tape. It can be anything fun.

After you create the game (you have five minutes), give it a name. Then, demonstrate the rules of the game or activity and how it would be played. Next, explore the following adaptations: How would you complete this with a group that had one kid who has the following condition?

1. deafness

2. blindness

3. short of breath

4. nervous and anxious

5. hyperactive

6. uses a wheelchair

7. deafness and blindness

See what you can do to change the game so each of the children are a real part of the activity. Use your creativity. In some rare instances, an activity may not be feasible or appropriate (e.g., pole vaulting for a person with quadriplegia). However, this should NOT be conceded until all possibilities have been tried and exhausted—remember, your box may be talking rather than reality.

Accessibility

One of the concerns a leader must think about when planning a program is accessibility. Accessibility is often thought of as focusing only on issues like ramps and railings for the person with a physical disability. Actually, the concept of accessibility is much bigger. It means being able to get to the door, through the door, to the second floor, and to participate, independently, and with dignity.

The ADA states that a public entity may comply with the accessibility requirement through many avenues. These include: redesign of equipment, assignment of aides to consumers, home visits, delivery of services at alternative accessible sites, alteration of existing facilities, construction of new facilities, use of accessible 'rolling stock' or other conveyances, or any other method. The bottom line is services, programs, and activities must be readily accessible to and usable by individuals with disabilities.

For the program planner understanding the basic concepts of accessibility is important. Specific dimensions and regulatory guidelines do not have to be memorized to be effective. All agencies should have a person in charge of architectural ADA access surveying. Contact them for more specific information.

Let's think of the whole recreation process and look at issues related to each step of leisure. A very brief look at access concerns follows:

1. **Getting information:** Do your agency and your program materials indicate accessibility? Are alternative types of public relations available (i.e., large print brochures)? See Public Relations (page 107) and Communication (page 64).

2. **Getting there:** Does your program provide or use a form of transportation (e.g., train, boat, bus, roller coaster)? If so, is it usable by a person who has impaired mobility?

3. **Signage:** Are handicap access symbols clearly visible from various entry points and at perimeters of your service areas?

4. **Parking:** Are there adequate handicapped parking spots available and are they well marked, near a curb cut, and within reasonable rolling distance to the entrance?

5. **Pathways:** Are the pathways to various points in your program maneuverable in a wheelchair? Are there tactile signs to assist someone with low vision? Are there hazards or obstructions that could cause safety problems?

6. **Seating:** Is there accessible seating available? Are these seats located in a variety of places to allow for closeness to friends and relatives, as well as price per seat diversity?

7. **Information Giving:** During the various aspects of a program, information is usually given in some manner. Can a person who cannot read, or cannot hear receive this information? This includes information in getting about the facility as well as instructional information. Symbols, braille and tactile, large print, audio and video information is useful. See Communication (page 64).

8. **Bathrooms:** Can a person using a wheelchair use the bathroom? Is it accessible with wide stalls, grab bars, and lower mounted equipment such as urinals, sinks and mirrors?

9. **Water Fountains, Phones, and Controls:** Can you use a phone or turn on the lights if you are short, in a wheelchair, or have poor hand use or a prosthesis?

Is there a TDD phone or relay service access nearby?

To condense all the issues of accessibility into an easy to remember slogan, the 4 S's of Super Access were invented.

Super Access 4-S System

Space, Safety, Seeking, and Sharing

1. **Space:** physical access related concerns.

2. **Safety:** safety concerns

3. **Seeking:** getting the information, assistance, funds, and support.

4. **Sharing:** networking.

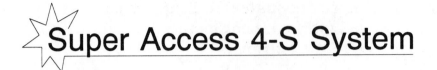

Super Access 4-S System

Space=physical access

- Accessibility is the key
  - Parking
  - Entry
  - Doors
- Bathrooms
  - Storage
  - Mobility
- Usability—phones, fountains, etc.

Safety=protection

- Hazard warnings
- Emergency alarms
- Evacuation plans
  - Staff training

Seeking=gathering

- Information
- Techniques/Adaptations
  - Experts
  - Funds
- Resources

Sharing=networking

- Ideas
- Inventions
- Successful processes
- Services available

Three formal guidelines for accessibility should be observed: (1) UFAS, Uniform Federal Accessibility Standards, (2) ADAAG, Americans with Disabilities Act Accessibility Guidelines, and (3) your State's Access Code.

Public Relations

Letting people know about recreation and leisure opportunities is a key to success. Now, think about how to let people with disabilities know about recreation opportunities and programs.

Printed Literature

Every agency should have an access statement. It should appear on every program specific brochure, flyer, or catalogue. A statement is being made that welcomes individuals with disabilities. It can be as simple as:

The _____ Parks and Recreation Division welcomes persons with disabilities in all programs and services. Please call us so that we will know how to best serve you. Our number is (916) 999-9999 Voice, (916) 999-9998 TDD.

Each program description and each program flyer should provide accurate accessibility information. If a building or service is not accessible, the alternative site should be indicated. If parts of a facility are not easily accessible or require advanced warning, such as rugged terrain, note this in advance in order to allow the person with a disability to make adequate decisions and plans before attending.

Have materials available in large print, audio cassette and braille. Additionally, picture/symbol communication and tactile representations are useful.

It is suggested that adaptive recreation programs be published in the general catalogue of services, and, then if desired, additionally in a separate format. Entries of accessible services can be made in local advocacy agency bulletins for cross advertising. See Resources (page 145) and Communication (page 64).

Registration

It is important to look at overall registration process and identify any barriers or potential areas of discrimination. There are many parts in the registration process. These include eligibility, registration forms, adaptive registration processes, and fees as they relate to the ADA.

Eligibility

Every program has eligibility criteria, whether formally or informally enforced. Youth sport leagues are an example. How is it decided that an adolescent makes the team and who makes that decision? The same questions apply to the level of team. This is not always a clear process.

The ADA makes subjective entrance requirements illegal. These are requirements that readily discriminate against a person with a disability. The law does state, however, that neutral rules and criteria that screen out individuals based on eligibility requirements are allowed. For example, there would be a necessary level of swimming required for safe participation in a high risk raft trip. These requirements must be based on actual safety risk prevention, and not on speculation.

The law refers to the concept of essential eligibility. This means the actual criteria needed to enter the program. Individuals with disabilities must meet the same predetermined essential eligibility criteria for a program that all participants must meet. The elements of essential eligibility may include:

1. **Capacity.** This means the number of persons allowed as maximum. For example, you have an aerobics class of 30 maximum size, and John would like to enter, do you allow him? If your answer is, "Yes, if he does not have a disability," then you are discriminating. Cutoff points are enforced regardless of disability. Cutoff points have nothing to do with disability. A person with a disability, who did not make the cutoff point, is not provided any special privileges. An evaluation of how one gets to enter very popular or overbooked programs needs to be done. Often the process includes some element of test of strength and stamina. This would be considered discriminatory.

2. **Charges.** Does the registrant have the cash, check, or credit card? Does the process demand a specific form of identification for payment like a drivers license? This could be discriminating if it excludes those who are unable to secure a limited source of identification or payment due to a disability or disability related issues. This does not mean that a person does not have to pay for services, but rather that it could be discriminatory to a person living on a fixed income due to a legal disability to be required to pay by credit card and/or offer credit card as security for equipment rental.

3. **Conduct.** Does the program have clear rules of conduct in writing? They should include a step-by-step account of the process of enforcement if rules are not met. All staff, volunteers, and contractual instructors should be trained and aware of rules of conduct. Consumers should be informed of these rules of conduct. Enforcement must be consistent and nonselective, not single out a person who has a disability. The law does request accommodation if the behaviors are due to a specific disability. For example, some individuals may have tics, or behaviors they cannot control. See Inappropriate Behaviors (page 88).

4. **Relative or Prerequisite Skill.** Some programs have prerequisite or relative skill requirements, others do not. Proof of passing a certain test, such as basic first aid before entering the advanced course, or a try-out in order to determine skill level are two common ways of testing prerequisite skills. The criteria must be formalized and enforced across the board with all people regardless of ability (or disability status).

   If a person does not possess the prerequisite skills needed to enter the program, they should be referred to a developmental level class or learning situation in order to upgrade necessary skills. Consider adding this type of program to existing offerings. Beware of irrelevant extraneous requirements, such as "must be able to understand verbal language" to join a dance class. Watching and doing may be an alternative way of following directions.

5. **Safety and Risk Management.** Program policies must clearly state that if a person's conduct poses physical harm, risk to self or others, they will be excluded from the program. Accommodation is mandated by the ADA. If their conduct is due to their disability, reasonable accommodation must first be provided. Methods such

as increased staffing (one-to-one), staff training, or calling in a consultant to assist with behavior problem management must be tried. Only following attempted and failed accommodation may a person be excluded from a program.

Eligibility information adapted from: John N. McGovern, *The Americans with Disabilities Act: A Challenge for California Park and Recreation Agencies Workshop Manual* (Sacramento, CA: California Park and Recreation Society, 1992) p. C-1&2.

Registration Forms

It is important to look at the registration process and begin to think about gathering information on accommodations. It is not proper to require information about a disability in an interview or registration form. It is fine to inquire if accommodations are needed, and to ask a person to volunteer specific needs, and concerns, and disabilities.

This means that sign up forms will need to have a section related to special needs. It can be as simple as:

"If you have any special needs due to a condition or
limitation, please explain:"

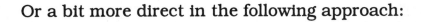
Or a bit more direct in the following approach:

Please indicate your need for any special accommodations related to a condition or limitation: Circle the aides that are appropriate and provide any further information you wish.

1. Sign language interpreter

2. Special diet (please explain)

3. Mobility guide

4. Accessible transportation (if transportation is an function of the program)

5. Special supervision needs, please explain:

6. Medication effects we should know about:

7. Any potential medical problems, such as allergies, seizures, fatigue, low blood sugar, or other conditions that we may need to know about:

8. Any potential safety problems we may need to know about, such as disorientation, etc.?

9. Need for adaptive devices/equipment? Please explain:

10. Other

The more information you provide, the better we will be able to serve you. Thank you for your cooperation.

Adaptive Processes

The registration process must be available to all. Think about the Communication section and apply this learning. It is suggested that registration be available in all forms of multimodal communication, from braille and large print to an instructional video with captions. Additionally, program selection, registration, and placement in a program may be best facilitated with a personal interview. Having a picture interest or program offerings book, with clear visuals of opportunities and a pictorial instructional guide to the registration processes will assist those with language differences. Having tactile representation of activities (e.g., sample art projects, sample equipment used) will assist those who use touch as their main source of information and program selection, such as individuals who have both hearing and visual impairments. Having a sign language interpreter available at peak registration hours for use by those who use sign would be ideal. Staff who process registration can begin to gear up by learning American sign language (ASL) as well as becoming aware of and familiar with other adaptive communication modes. See Communication (page 64).

Fees

In today's world, fees are a reality. People with disabilities have the right to be treated with fairness and respect. Paying their own way is part of that.

However, the reality is that most people with disabilities live on very limited incomes, often from a state fund that is very unpredictable in these days of budget problems. A person with this type of income often has less than $20 of discretionary income per month. This goes for clothes, and a hamburger out, and recreation fees. If the program fee is $45 for a 5-week ceramics class, the consumer may not have the total fee that month. A fee structure system that allows time payments is one possible accommodation. Another is fundraising and sponsorship efforts to support various consumers who have proven economic hardships with your fee-based programs.

If a person with a disability has the need for a personal attendant or aide in order participate in the program, the aide should not have to pay a fee for the program. The aide is really working to allow the consumer to play. It is reasonable to asses the attendant's real costs such as meals during the program, if he/she chooses to partake. Some agencies may decide to cover these minimal extra costs.

The law clearly prohibits placing a surcharge on a particular individual with a disability or on any group of individuals with disabilities, to cover any costs or measures required to provide that individual or group with the nondiscriminatory treatment required by the ADA.

Additional Staff

The ADA clearly states that auxiliary aids, including extra staff, are the responsibility of the program or service. In some instances, a recreation program has required a group of participants with disabilities to bring their own staff, counselors or aides as a requirement of participation. This is like the school that will allow students to come, if they bring their own teacher. These types of arrangements have to be reexamined.

If a consumer evidences a need for more intensive staff supervision than is usually provided, there are several ways to approach the situation:

1. **Assign an extra staff member.** Instruct him/her to focus on upgrading the skills of the consumer with disabilities and assist with integration.

2. **Develop a leisure buddy system.** These have proven to be highly successful. A leisure buddy is a screened and trained volunteer who acts as a friend and coplayer to the consumer. He/she is usually matched on similar leisure interests.

3. **Develop a leisure coach system.** Leisure coaches are also screened and trained volunteers. They commit to actually teaching a leisure or socialization skill to the consumer.

4. **Involve community groups.** If a club, organization, business, or group can be involved, staff ratio will improve.

5. **Involve students.** Students (high school, college, and university) often get credit for volunteering through classes, practicums and internships. They can come from a wide variety of disciplines and provide needed assistance.

A word about personal care attendants (PCAs). The ADA clearly states that personal care (i.e., feeding, toileting, and changing clothing) is not required to be performed by your staff unless customarily provided (28 CFR, 36.303). There are several ways to approach this. (1) Do it anyway in certain circumstances (e.g., the swim program where your staff regularly helps young children with getting dressed, if needed. (2) Offer the service by your staff for a reasonable fee (portion of hourly wage needed to complete tasks). (3) Allow a sibling or friend to attend and assist without a program fee (28 CFR, 35.135). (4) Allow a counselor or PCA to attend without program fees unless the fee includes direct costs such as meals (28 CFR, 35.135).

A qualified staff is the key. Training is needed for ALL staff, paid and unpaid. Many programs today rely on volunteer staff. It is extremely important to train these volunteers. Each agency must provide a safe, fun, and accessible program for all consumers.

PEOPLE RESOURCES ARE THE KEY!

ADA and Risk Management Plans

How do employees fit into the total picture of ADA compliance and risk management? Each agency varies greatly, so it is only possible to offer general information regarding these important components.

Fitting Into The ADA Plan

Each person in an agency is responsible for making sure that his/her aspect of service provision is making reasonable accommodations for individuals with disabilities. Getting information and acting upon it is the key. Each agency is required by law to appoint a designated ADA coordinator (an individual responsible for overall ADA compliance). This person is in charge of coordinating all ADA efforts including:

access surveys, agency self-assessment, transition plans for improvements, and a consumer complaint system. Identify the ADA officer within the agency. He/she can be called upon for assistance, to answer questions, and to make referrals and recommendations.

Fitting Into Your Risk Management Plan

Each employee in an agency is also an integral part of a safety and risk management plan. The risk management plan will have to be reexamined with regard to policies, procedures, new equipment or services related to ADA compliance. This plan is usually formally developed, with an appointed officer or someone who is in charge. Some of the elements that are critical to this plan include:

1. Adequate supervision

2. Skill development opportunities

3. Informing consumer of potential risks

4. Assumption of risk forms

5. Safe conditions

6. Skill grouping of participants

7. Waiver forms

8. Proper use of equipment

9. First aid

10. Knowing abilities and limitations of consumers

Safety, risk management, and the provision of quality leisure services go hand in hand with ADA compliance. Identify the ADA and risk management officers of the agency. Get to know them and your agency's legal representative. Invite them to attend programs. Ask for their input and assistance when needed as you implement new strategies, purchase new equipment, or train new staff, etc. Provide them with input and feedback on policies, processes and programs related to ADA compliance.

Human Service Professionals Who Facilitate Integrated Services For Individuals With Disabilities Will Want To:

- Understand normalization and human dignity principals.

- Know the legislative basis for integration.

- Serve as an advocate; speak out and ask, "Where are consumers with disabilities?"

- Act as a facilitator of service access for *all* people.

- Advocate for accessibility modifications.

- Adapt public relations to multimode sources (e.g., audiotape, large print, braille, symbol language, sign language).

- Indicate with a brief statement (e.g., "Our services are accessible to people with disabilities—for further information call 555-6055 or TDD-6056.")

- Develop specialized public relations efforts with agencies dealing with special populations specifically.

- Assure nonlabelistic, nonhandicapped, public relations efforts for all community public relations.

- Train *all* personnel in normalization, integration, communication, helpful hints and attitudes related to individuals with disabilities.

- Coordinate volunteer efforts to facilitate participation.

- Arrange transportation systems (e.g., public bus, travel training programs, ride sharing).

- Coordinate adaptive equipment access (i.e., rental, loan, equipment, pool, and/or interagency sharing).

- Arrange fee alternative if needed (e.g., long-term payments, prorated by income fees, work-energy exchanges, sponsorship).

- Arrange for any specialized service through regular department responsible for the service (e.g., childcare, dietary needs, attendant care, interpreter).

- Promote hiring people with disabilities.

- Involve people with disabilities in *all* phases of program or service planning, delivery, and evaluation.

6

Common Disability Categories

The following chapter contains basic information about various common disabilities including:

- General Terminology

- Acquired Immune Deficiency Syndrome (AIDS)

- Chemical Dependency/Substance Abuse

- Developmental Disabilities

- Diabetes

- Eating Disorders

- Epilepsy

- Head Injuries

- Hearing or Auditory Impairment

- Hemophilia

- Mental Health Problems and Psychiatric Disorders

- Multiple Disabilities

- Physical Disabilities

- Visual Impairment

- A Special Note On Individuals Who Are Older

- Resources Utilized in Disability Categories Section

The information provided on disability categories is not meant to be comprehensive in any way. It is only an overview.

A recreation professional encounters people with many different types of disabilities. It is impossible to name each type and all the ramifications. This is an overview of some common disabling conditions and some of the things that relate to recreation accommodations for these disabilities.

General Terminology

The onset or beginning of a disability affects the style of adjustment a person may have. *Congenital* means that a person is born with the disability. *Adventitious* means that the disability is due to an accident or event later in life. *Degenerative* means the condition worsens over time. *Chronic* means it may come and go, but cannot be cured. *Temporary* means having a short duration. *Permanent* means just the opposite, forever. These are adjectives that are used along with names of disabilities. Example: She has a degenerative heart condition that is permanent. *Diagnosis* is a medically determined problem. *Prognosis* is the potential predicted future outcomes related to the disability. *Etiology* is the background, cause or reason for the problem, if determinable.

The term *differential diagnosis* simply means that each person with a specific type of disability is not like one with a similar diagnosis. Each person will have different problems, solutions, and adaptations. One cannot assume that a person with Down syndrome is like every other person with Down syndrome.

Explaining each disability category is a difficult task. The material covered is a general introduction to basic types of disability. Consider the helpful programming hints that relate to each category.

Remember, these categories are conditions, just like having blond(e) hair. They are only one part of a person, not the whole person. They are not to be used as labels, rather only as information. They should be left out when addressing the consumer or referring to him/her.

Acquired Immune Deficiency Syndrome (AIDS)

Acquired Immune Deficiency Syndrome is a disease that effects the body's ability to fight off infection (*What Young People Should Know about AIDS*, 1990). The human immunodeficiency virus (HIV) is the virus that attacks the immune system and may lead to full blown AIDS. This is when the immune system is determined to be below a certain level as marked by specific measures of antibodies. Individuals with HIV is the term used to indicate that a person has tested HIV-positive, but is not yet not facing the symptoms of AIDS.

Helpful Hints:

1. *Know the facts about AIDS and HIV infection.* It is **not casually transmitted** through hand shakes, hugs, conversation, or the use of common shower or toilet facilities.

2. Understand that in a public setting, the person with AIDS or HIV is at a higher risk of catching a cold which could lead to more serious problems, than someone would be at risk of catching AIDS.

3. Honor possible staff apprehension and get training in the subject for them.

4. People with HIV infection may be taking medication that affects their energy levels. Nausea and fatigue are common side effects of AIDS medications.

5. Today a person with AIDS may live many years without significant health problems, and leisure contributes to longevity. It is a basic human right to have leisure.

6. If a medical emergency should arise, be prepared with an approved safety/first-aid plan. Ask a consulting nurse and local AIDS information group for the latest proper techniques. Rubber gloves are now suggested for first-aid situations as precautionary measures.

Chemical Dependency/Substance Abuse

The prolonged consumption of excessive amounts of a chemical including alcohol, drugs, nicotine, caffeine, and/or food substances. This leads to severe psychological and physical dependency on the chemical, and often results in physical, mental, emotional, and social problems (Austin & Crawford, 1991). The most common types of chemical dependencies are smoking, alcohol, drugs, and eating disorders.

Alcohol

Helpful Hints:

1. A person who has spent a lot of time at leisure under the influence of alcohol may lack sober leisure experiences, be unsure of himself/herself, or lacking leisure skills. See Working and Playing With Individuals With Learning Difference section (page 81).

2. Do not condone or promote alcohol consumption.

3. Choose settings and events that are not alcohol dependent. Make sure nonalcoholic beverages are available if it is an environment where alcohol may be served (a ball game or gambling trip). Consult with the consumer before going to any environment that may be serving alcohol.

4. Promote stress management and wellness activities.

Drugs

Helpful Hints:

1. Most recovering individuals will not be identifiable. Treat all individuals the same.

2. All individuals need to be steered away from others in the group that may idolize chemical use.

3. Be aware of the signs and symptoms of someone under the influence of illegal drugs. They include pinpoint or dilated eye pupils, lethargy, rapid talk, hypertension, dry mouth, bugged open eyes,

paranoid behavior, restlessness, constant trips to the restroom, continual sniffling, evidence of drug paraphernalia such as straws, vials, matchbook covers folded, medicinal or pot odors, and any pronounced change in mood or behavior. Note that some of these symptoms also accompany the use of legal drugs, so caution must be exercised in approaching a person regarding drug use. Do so privately and confidentially.

4. Know appropriate referrals to local agencies and self-help groups serving persons with chemical addictions.

5. According to the ADA, it is not your responsibility to serve someone who is actively using illegal drugs. Your duty as a professional is to provide an appropriate referral.

Developmental Disabilities (D.D.)

This is a broad category of conditions that have the potential of slowing or limiting a person's development (thus the title). The official definition of a developmental disability is as follows:

> A severe, chronic disability attributed to physical and/or mental impairment that develops before age 22, continues indefinitely, and causes limitations in three or more life areas such as language, mobility, and cognition (Grossman, 1983).

There are various types of disabilities that usually fall under the label of developmental disabilities. They are mental retardation, cerebral palsy, autism, and some specific learning disabilities. The term developmental disabilities covers disabilities that are focused on physical problems and others that are cognitive problems. Due to the uniqueness of each of the categories within this larger, catchall label, each is covered separately below:

Autism

A syndrome of early childhood characterized by (1) abnormal social relationships (usually shy of people contact), (2) language disorder with impaired understanding (often nonverbal), (3) rituals and compulsiveness,

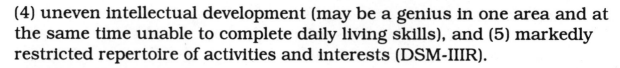

(4) uneven intellectual development (may be a genius in one area and at the same time unable to complete daily living skills), and (5) markedly restricted repertoire of activities and interests (DSM-IIIR).

Helpful Hints:

1. Allow the consumer time to adjust to a new environment. Orient him/her to the facility and area.

2. Allow for progressive involvement in social activities like being in a room with other people before being asked to play a team game.

3. Allow for partial participation, meaning being in the game for a few minutes and then being able to float around and watch.

4. Honor their form of communication, drawing, speaking, gestures and body language.

5. Try to understand what motivates them and use this as behavior reinforcement. If a person likes to swim and the prerequisite is to listen to instructions, the reward is natural—the pool.

6. Remember, attention spans may be shorter than average. Allow for diverse tasks and activities within one program hour. At the same time require longer attention as the person adjusts to the activity.

7. Develop a program policy plan to manage disruptive behaviors and use this in an equitable way with all participants.

8. Determine if the person has community safety skills through supervised observation. If they seem unsafe, be sure to provide close supervision for this person.

For further hints see *Working and Playing With Individuals With Learning Differences* (page 81).

Cerebral Palsy Syndromes (C.P.)

A loose descriptive term that is applied to a number of nonprogressive motor disorders resulting from damage to the central nervous system. Usually congenital and characterized by loss or impairment of control of voluntary muscle movements (Goldenson, 1978).

There are various classifications of Cerebral Palsy (C.P.):

Spastic Syndromes—(most common) Tight muscles and movement in a variety of degrees, from hemiplegia (one side of body, arms and legs), paraplegia (lower extremities), or quadriplegia (all four quadrants of body, legs and arms).

Athetosis—A condition, chiefly in children, of slow involuntary writhing, floppy movements of the fingers, toes, hands and feet.

Ataxia—Loss of coordination of the muscles, especially, the extremities, causing uneven walking gait, and difficulty with rapid or fine movements.

Mixed Forms—A mixture of types from above.

Helpful Hints:

1. Some people with cerebral palsy will use assistive devices like wheelchairs and canes, so be prepared to make arrangements. See Wheelchairs and Devices, page 82)

2. Because of poor muscle control, verbal language may be slow, different, or not feasible. Be patient, and do not speak for them. Note if communication boards or augmented communication devices are used. See Communication (page 64).

3. Water is very freeing and pools are best kept heated to assist in relaxing muscles.

4. Do not lift a person with cerebral palsy under their arms; this may cause a spastic reaction.

5. Jerky motions may create a problem in activities such as board games. Adaptations such as card holders, games with pegged in markers and larger size chips/dice or paint brush handles help the person with difficult fine motor (little muscles of fingers/hand) skills.

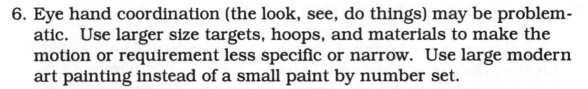

6. Eye hand coordination (the look, see, do things) may be problematic. Use larger size targets, hoops, and materials to make the motion or requirement less specific or narrow. Use large modern art painting instead of a small paint by number set.

7. Allow for both full and partial participation, or participation via verbal input on activities that may be beyond the person's physical abilities.

8. Do not assume that if a person has difficulty speaking that he/she does not understand language or that they think slowly. This is just a motor problem in most cases. Mental retardation is only found in a small percentage of people with cerebral palsy.

Mental Retardation

Subaverage (below 100 I.Q. on intelligence tests) intellectual ability, manifesting itself during the developmental years up to 22 years, accompanied by deficits in adaptive behavior in life areas such as communication, cognition, and socialization.

There are levels of mental retardation. They are determined by I.Q. ranges. They are provided here from the closest to normal I.Q. being :

1. Mildly Retarded

2. Moderately Retarded

3. Severely Retarded, and

4. Profoundly Retarded (Grossman, 1983).

It is this author's belief that identifying various characteristics of each type is slanderous. Training and education are intermediate factors contributing to what a person can and cannot do. In the past, we believed that individuals with moderate levels of mental retardation could not be educated (e.g., reading, writing), thus we never bothered to find out. Guess what? Many individuals can read, write, and learn a foreign language.

At levels 3 and 4, multiple impairments such as heart defects, hearing and visual problems, or epilepsy may be present. Down syndrome is a specific type of mental retardation. There are many other specific types of mental retardation.

Helpful Hints:

1. Many general guidelines are provided in the section on Workng and Playing With Individuals With Learning Differences (page 81).

2. Leisure exposure may have been limited, especially if the person has been living in an institution in the past. Present new, age appropriate activities in sequential processes. Teach all the skills (e.g., dress, equipment needed, rules—written and assumed, social and leisure skills). Ask, "How can I really assist this person to fit in and be successful at this activity?"

3. If working with a person with Down syndrome, a physician's permission must be obtained for him/her to participate in activities that may flex the neck because of a condition common to this disability called *atlantozxial instability*. If they have this, they most likely cannot swim or do gymnastics or other activities that require head twisting type movements (Project LIFE, 1988).

4. Social sexuality is often a concern for leaders. People with mental retardation may have less inhibitions and be forward in their expressions of caring. It is not against the law for teenagers or adults to express caring and affection. This often happens in a recreational setting. A general rule of thumb about these behaviors is to ask: If he/she were not retarded, would we allow this behavior? Treat him/her as you would anyone else. If a consumer is exhibiting inappropriate behavior, respectfully and confidentially—meaning alone and not in front of anyone—tell them to cool it. Show them more acceptable ways of expressing affection in public. There are programs utilizing videos and slides that help teach social sexual skills to people with learning differences. See Resources (page 145).

Learning Disabilities

People with learning disabilities have average or above average intelligence, but they experience difficulties in processing information related to spoken or written language. This results in reading, writing, spelling, math, speaking, and coordination problems due to perceptual problems. Each person has a different type and degree of learning disability (Goldenson, 1978).

Helpful Hints:

1. See *Learning Differences*.

2. If your program involves written instructions, be sure to interpret verbally also.

3. Avoid putting the person on the spot. Example: asking an adolescent to fill out a long registration form, or a writing type activity. Asking for an impromptu answer to a question in front of a large group may cause embarrassment. These are situations that require extra time for a person with a learning disability due to processing difficulties.

4. In a school setting the kinds of accommodations that are provided for students include: oral papers or exams, extended or nontimed test limits, interpreters and transcribers for tests and note taking, and audiotaped books. Time management and stress management are also emphasized to help with organization. These techniques, creatively applied, can be inserted into a recreation program.

5. Some people with learning disabilities have poor coordination, thus safety situations must be analyzed (e.g., walking a log to cross the river).

Diabetes

Formally called *diabetes mellitus*, diabetes is a syndrome arising from an inadequate production or utilization of body insulin (Austin, D., Therapeutic Recreation Processes and Techniques, 1991). Insulin is critical for the body to process (or metabolize) blood sugar or glucose. Hyperglycemia, or having too much blood sugar, is a major problem of the person with diabetes. Two types of diabetes exist. Type I called insulin-dependent diabetes is monitored by the person taking artificial sources of insulin via injections or medications. Type II, or noninsulin-dependent diabetes, is when some insulin is manufactured by the body, but the insulin level is insufficient to counter the amount of sugars that need to be processed, therefore, monitoring food intake (both type and quantity) is necessary to monitor blood sugar levels (American Diabetes

Association, 1987). The following symptoms are typical, but each person has a unique set of symptoms. However, some people with noninsulin-dependent diabetes have symptoms so mild they go unnoticed.

Insulin-dependent (usually occur suddenly)	**Noninsulin-dependent** (usually occur less suddenly)
• frequent urination • excessive thirst • extreme hunger • dramatic weight loss • irritability • weakness or fatigue • nausea and vomiting	• any of the insulin-dependent symptoms • hard-to-heal skin, gum, or bladder infections • drowsiness • blurred vision • tingling or numbness in hands or feet • itching

Helpful Hints:

1. Know the first-aid steps for hypoglycemia (too little blood sugar) because this is a life threatening situation and does require immediate treatment with glucose. A hypoglycemia problem may occur due to overmedication, if too little food is eaten, if a meal is delayed, or due to an unusual amount of energy expenditure. For instance, a day long hike or exhausting game of basketball, or when regular meals and healthy snacks have been skipped.

   When a person is experiencing hypoglycemic reactions they may feel cold, clammy, nervous, shaky, weak, or very hungry. Some people become pale, get headaches, or act strangely (become disoriented, moody or experience thought pattern changes), and in extreme cases, become unconscious. You will want to administer glucose if they are conscious and can swallow.

   Sources of Glucose: Any quick acting glucose such as glucose tablets, orange juice (8 ounces), nondiet cola (8 ounces), corn syrup (1 Tablespoon), honey (1 Tablespoon), candy bar (1 ounce), or hard candy (6 small pieces).

   If a person becomes unconscious, glucagon, a hormone (available by prescription only) that raises blood sugar, must be injected.

2. It is sometimes hard to tell if a person is having hyperglycemia (too much sugar) or hypoglycemia. Administering glucose as stated above will not hurt if it is hyperglycemia, but will be critical if it is hypoglycemia. It is best to err on the side of administering glucose, since failure to treat a hypoglycemic episode can lead to serious health complications and even death (Austin, 1991).

Hyperglycemia occurs when too much food is eaten and not enough insulin is taken. The warning signs are large amounts of sugar in the urine and blood, frequent urination, excessive thirst, and nausea. High blood sugar should be treated with the help of a doctor. Ketoacidosis, or diabetic coma, may accompany hyperglycemia. This condition usually takes several hours or days, and can be brought under control at the first signs of hyperglycemia. In addition to high blood- and urine-sugar tests, the symptoms include dry mouth, great thirst, loss of appetite, excessive urination, dry and flushed skin, labored breathing, fruity-smelling breath, and possibly vomiting, abdominal pain, and unconsciousness. This condition is usually found in people with insulin-dependent diabetes.

3. It is very helpful to know a little about the person who has diabetes in your program, including a medical information involving what type of diabetes they have and what types management they require with meals, snacks and exercise they utilize, as well as gain an understanding of the medications they may take. This, of course, is a private issue and may or may not be disclosed by the person. It is their choice. It is a matter of rapport and tact to approach a person politely and respectfully.

When offering meal accommodations with a program, one should always include a question asking for dietary restrictions within the registration form. A line as simple as "Please inform us of any dietary restrictions below" would allow your organization to be informed across the board about *everyone* within the group including people with food allergies/sensitivities.

4. It is also helpful to understand what types of symptoms a person may experience when and if they ever do have problems with hypoglycemia or hyperglycemia. Again, you can inquire tactfully providing the person with an option for answering or not answering.

5. When meals or refreshments are part of your programs and services, move towards the healthy, nonsugary types of options. Fresh fruits, vegetables, whole grain pasta, breads, and legumes are beneficial for all people. Sweet desserts, if absolutely called for, need to have a complementary type of nonsugar option. There are nonsugar (dietetic) ice creams, cakes, candies, and other options available commercially.

6. If you are sponsoring a day long or overnight event, avoid skipping meals or altering meal schedules radically.

7. Be aware that moderate exercise is vital for the person with diabetes. However, if a person expends more energy than usual, they will be at risk to be imbalanced with their food intake and energy expenditure, and will possibly need to supplement their intake with a healthy snack.

8. Due to poor circulation and other problems that may accompany diabetes, it is critical to monitor any bruises, cuts or abrasions carefully. It is very important to remind participants to wear hardy footwear and protective clothing, and to regularly check their feet and lower extremities for any signs of problems. OBTAIN MEDICAL CONSULTATION if any signs of redness, blisters, pain, swelling, or a break in the skin are found (Austin, 1991).

Eating Disorders

People with eating disorders have psychological problems and use eating as a solution to personality deficits that include low self-esteem, trust and autonomy. Anorexia nervosa (extreme undereating), bulimia (the binge and purge dieter) and a mixture, called bulimarexia, are the most common types of eating disorders.

1. Activities that promote health, balance in life, and self-esteem should be emphasized. Most people with eating disorders need total acceptance and unconditional positive regard.

2. Often an abnormal focus on weight loss will limit activity choices to those which can burn calories. Promote *moderate* involvement in exercise, and attempt to broaden interests to other areas such as art and culture.

3. Anticipate situations where food may be a part of the activity, and be sure the person knows in advance. Try to avoid a food focus in activities.

4. Note any undereating or overeating (meaning in exaggerated quantities). Also watch for excessive and prolonged visits to the restroom after meals. These are signs of anorexia nervousa, bulimia, or bulimarexia.

5. Be informed of local support groups and mental health referrals.

Epilepsy

A disorder of the nervous system usually characterized by convulsions or attacks leading to loss of consciousness. There are a variety of types of epilepsy including:

1. **Grand Mal**—Sudden loss of consciousness, followed by muscular spasms of whole body. Frothing of the mouth, and incontinence may occur. Attacks usually last 2-5 minutes. Person is very tired afterwards.

2. **Petite Mal**—A shorter type of seizure, usually under a minute, that involves only parts of the body and, perhaps the head (eyes, mouth twitching).

Helpful Hints:

1. The main concern for a recreator is the person's safety if a state of unconsciousness should occur. Swimming, rock climbing and individual high risk sports such as kayaking and horseback riding need to be considered with a plan for "what if?" This does not always mean limiting participation, just being prepared. Buddy systems are very useful in these situations.

2. Some environments may exaggerate the potential of seizures. Flashing lights, loud music, certain sounds and visuals may trigger seizures in individuals. Ask the consumer if he/she experiences any triggers.

3. Fatigue may also exaggerate seizures. Watch for signs of tiredness and assist the consumer in self-seizure control by regulating rest periods in physical activities.

4. Social stigma is a concern. Be sure to be confidential about your knowledge of a person's condition (this goes for all disabilities).

5. If a seizure should occur, KNOW WHAT TO DO! See page 89.

Head Injuries

Head injury, sometimes referred to as brain injury, is a traumatic insult to the brain of a degenerative or congenital nature that may produce a diminished or altered state of consciousness (Adams & McCubbin, 1991). This results in physical, intellectual, emotional, and social changes in the individual because the brain controls all functions. There are several types of head injury including: closed head injury (e.g., whip lashed and torqued brain from a car accident), and; open head injury (gunshot wound). Traumatic head injury may occur from a stroke, drowning, or other accidents causing a lack of oxygen.

The effects of a head injury vary tremendously and depend on the area of the brain damaged, the severity of damage, and the length of time spent in a coma. Common functional limitations include short and long-term memory loss, communication difficulties such as word finding, logic and reasoning difficulties, various physical disabilities including hemiplegia, ineffective social skills, and accompanying emotional problems such as anger and depression.

Helpful Hints:

1. Memory is usually a problem, so a person may have to relearn many of his/her leisure skills.

2. Repetition is necessary for learning as well as reinforcement. See Working and Playing With Individuals With Learning Differences (page 81).

3. Frustration may be very real. Allow extra time, noncompetitive activities, and expression of feelings.

4. Invent ways to provide cues and reminders for the client in a program via instructional handouts, visual sequences of activities and models to look at.

5. Structure and organization is necessary for success. This person may need external sources as well as internal sources (from within). A direct leadership style which offers choices such as, "Select from these two colors of paint" rather than a do what you want style of instruction will be useful.

6. Often the person with a head injury carries a daily journal, calendar, and reminder book. Assist in reminding him/her to make entries and notes about what has transpired and future events and instructions.

7. Do not assume that verbal information is remembered. A call and a written reminder may be necessary regarding your program needs.

8. Judgement may be faulty and safety concerns must be analyzed. Closely supervise until you know the consumer's capabilities.

9. Some people may have fragile skulls and need to use helmets at all times and avoid any activity that would potentially lead to any physical blows or excess pressure to the head (yoga head stands or fast-pitch baseball).

10. Some people may use adaptive equipment due to physical limitations resulting from the head injury. See Wheelchairs and Devices (page 82).

Hearing or Auditory Impairment

Hearing loss ranges from mild to moderate hearing impairment to total deafness. Three types of hearing loss include conductive hearing impairments due to problems in the mechanisms of the auditory canal and middle ear, and sensorineural loss, associated with a lesion or problem with the inner ear and auditory nerves. Central hearing loss means a person can hear, but cannot understand what he hears, as in the case of a person with a stroke (Adams & McCubbin, 1991).

The major limitations a person with a hearing impairment faces is communication. Speech and language, both coming in (receptive) and going out (expressive) may be difficult. Often it is the person without the hearing impairment who has the problem, as he/she may not know sign language while the person with deafness does. People with hearing impairments may use voice, lip reading, sign language, gestures, writing, and communication devices for communication.

Helpful Hints:

1. Safety may be a concern in some recreational environments that lend themselves to unexpected events. An example: While camping, you cannot yell at a child who has deafness to watch out for the snake. Buddy systems help in these situations.

2. Some types of hearing impairments affect the inner ear and thus balance. This is a consideration when doing activities requiring balance.

3. Develop a safety or danger alert signal. For example, flash the lights to warn individuals with hearing impairments as needed.

4. Acquire the services of a certified interpreter for events, meetings, classes, and activities for participants who have deafness and use sign language. Registration forms should have a check box for requested interpreter services. It is not necessary to have an interpreter at each program, only if requested.

5. As a leader, learn some basic sign language and finger spelling.

6. Encourage other staff and participants to learn also.

7. Be sure that participants with hearing impairments are situated in front and close to the action so they can see the face and hands of the leader or performer.

8. Try to limit distractions (auditory and movement) when presenting information.

9. Use brief, clear and simple language when using notes or instruction. Some individuals do not read or write English at a high level because American Sign Language, does not closely follow English grammar. It is more like German in its style. Example: An English

sentence would be, "I am going to the store." In sign language it would come out as, "I store go." So written language may resemble this style.

10. Be patient and willing to communicate. ***Do not fake it if you do not understand.***

11. Showing as well as explaining will help.

12. Augmented listening devices (little microphones and headphones) can be easily purchased and provided to amplify classes and events for individuals with hearing impairments.

13. Know where the most accessible TDD phone is and the number of the local relay system.

For further information, consult Communication (page 64).

Hemophilia

Hemophilia is a bleeding disorder, usually affecting males, that results in prolonged bleeding, primarily into muscles or joints. It is reassuring to know that people with hemophilia do not bleed any faster than people whose blood clots normally. They may, however, bleed longer unless they receive appropriate treatment. There are three levels of hemophilia—mild, moderate, and severe. The person with mild hemophilia may only have prolonged bleeding during things like surgeries or major injuries. The person with severe hemophilia may have frequent bleeding episodes, some of them from no apparent trauma. Fortunately, with all types, bleeding can be controlled with current medical treatment. For most people with hemophilia, blood clotting factor is the key to resolving prolonged bleeding episodes (Beiersdorfer, 1991).

Helpful Hints:

1. Know proper first aid. When a person with hemophilia sustains an injury, the primary first-aid procedure provided should be identical to everyone else. It may, however, need to be followed by an intravenous infusion of the clotting factor. Many people self-administer their infusion. Only trained individuals should administer the treatment.

2. As with all first aid today, using protective rubber gloves and anti-septic is critical to help stop transmission of infection. HIV infection is now a part of the realities that face some individuals with hemophilia due to blood transfusions received before blood was routinely screened for HIV.

3. An injury to the head, neck or abdomen could lead to internal bleeding that may go undetected. It is critical to SEEK MEDICAL ATTENTION if this happens (National Hemophilia Foundation, 1990).

4. Think "Safeguard the Environment." A nail, tack, or other unseen object poses problems. Take a look around and carefully inspect by both observation and tactile analysis for any potential source of unwanted cuts or scrapes in and around your place of program.

5. At times, protective clothing, such as a helmet, reinforced or padded clothing are important safety measures to utilize.

6. Regular exercise is important for a person with hemophilia, however, ALL CONTACT SPORTS SHOULD BE AVOIDED.

Mental Health Problems and Psychiatric Disorders

People with mental health problems are no longer called mentally ill because of the stigma. The term is a person with a psychiatric or mental disorder. This condition is not mental retardation, a common mistake. Mental disorders are difficult to define—yet suggest a lack of mental health or the general ability to cope with life stresses (Austin & Crawford, 1991). Mental disorders can be defined as:

> An illness with psychological or behavioral manifestations and/or impairment in functioning due to social, psychological, genetic, physical/chemical, or biological disturbances. There are many types of mental disorders including psychoses, mood disorders, anxiety disorders, and personality disorders.

Mental disorders may be short term or chronic (over long periods of time). The degree and severity of the problem varies greatly as does the adaptation of the individual to the problem. One in every ten persons will face a mental health problem at one point in their lives. Mental health problems are probably the least understood and least talked about disability, yet they are common to all of us, in some way through ourselves, family, and friends.

Classifications of mental disorders include:

1. **Personality Disorders**—Often rigid and maladaptive behaviors. Within this category there is paranoid (suspicious attitude), schizoid (withdrawn, self-absorbed), antisocial (disregards rules, law, others), borderline personality (frequent mood shifts, impulsiveness, intense anger), dependent (low self-esteem, helpless behaviors), compulsive (perfectionist, orderly, inflexible), and passive-aggressive (clinging, procrastination, avoids responsibility, superficial compliance).

2. **Mood Disorders**—Sustained problems with depression and/or elation. There are two types including: Bipolar characterized by alternating cycles of depression and elation, and unipolar characterized by depression, agitation, weight loss or gain, guilt, and loss of capacity to experience pleasure.

3. **Schizophrenic Disorders**—Generally chronic, resulting in disturbances in thinking, feeling and behavior.

4. **Anxiety Disorders**—Characterized by feelings of nervousness, anxiety, and sometimes panic attacks.

Helpful Hints:

1. Some people with mental health problems may have learning problems due to low motivation, depression and drug induced drowsiness. See Learning Differences (page 81) for useful hints.

2. Various drugs that are used to treat mental health problems may cause side effects such as motor tremors, slurred speech, and extreme sensitivity to the sun. Of course, it is not advisable to mix any drug with alcohol.

3. General rules for persons on mental health medications: NO ALCOHOL, LIMIT CAFFEINE, LIMIT SUN EXPOSURE WITH HATS AND SUN BLOCK. PROVIDE PLENTY OF WATER AND FREQUENT RESTROOM STOPS.

4. If you are going on a day trip or overnight program, review the necessary drug regime with the consumer and or care provider. It is NOT a recreation leader's responsibility to distribute medications; however, he/she can provide schedule reminders.

5. Keep in mind that a person may have some learning difficulties but is NOT retarded. Keep adult level interaction appropriate.

6. Some cognitive skills may have been misplaced due to a mental problem. Reading and writing skills once known may be forgotten or resemble skills of those with learning disabilities.

7. The types of assistance offered a person with a mental disorder in colleges today are the same as those provided a person with a learning disability. They are things like nontimed tests, readers and transcribers, audiotaped books and materials, and instructions given using multimodal techniques. You'll want to consider these accommodations for your recreation programs.

8. Make allowances for actions that are really not disruptive to the activity or harmful to self or others. Everyone does not have to be or act the same.

9. Provide opportunities for success. Give leadership and planning responsibilities whenever possible.

10. Use reasonable behavior management techniques if behavior is inappropriate and not acceptable. See Inappropriate Behaviors (page 88).

11. Develop and consistently implement a neutral policy on conduct and behavior for programs, and enforce it equitably.

12. Seek assistance from a qualified mental health professional or appropriate agency as needed.

Multiple Disabilities

A person having more than one disability. The combinations are limitless. An example would be a person who has deafness and blindness. Another would be a person with diabetes and a visual impairment, or how about a person with Down syndrome, heart problems, and low vision. A recent example is a person with Down syndrome at birth who now faces Alzheimer's disease later in life.

Basically a person with multiple disabilities faces the challenges of each disability and some compounding effect from the combination of the conditions.

Helpful Hints:

1. Get to know the person. See the sections that pertain, e.g., Working and Playing With Indiviuals With Learning Differences (page 81), Wheelchairs and Devices (page 82), Inappropriate Behaviors (page 88).

2. Learning about the separate disabilities of a person lends only a partial picture of who a person is. Personal characteristics and disability characteristics combine to create a unique individual.

3. For a person with severe multiple disabilities, such as quadriplegia and head injury, partial participation may be appropriate. For example, the participant in a CPR class would verbally instruct another to complete the procedures for them. The same would hold true for playing a game of chess.

Physical Disabilities

There are thousands of specific physical disabilities. Information about them could and does fill many books. People with physical disabilities are often referred to as individuals who are physically disabled, physically challenged, or physically handicapped. This is out of date. Remember that individuals do not *become* a disability—individuals have a disability. The correct terminology is individual with a physical disability.

Some physical disabilities are invisible, such as heart disease or diabetes. Others are very visible such as a person who has been burned or a person missing a leg due to amputation.

Helpful Hints:

1. Ask the person what assistance is needed. Do not assume assistance is needed. Although daily living assistance such as feeding and toileting is not required to be provided by recreation agencies by the ADA, it is not against the law to do so, by any means, and certainly should be considered.

2. Be creative. Do not look at what a person cannot do, like walking, but rather the *real requirement* of the activity, like getting to first base by any way possible. See Program Adaptations (page 97).

3. Know how to properly assist a person using a wheelchair, cane, or gurney. See Wheelchairs and Devices (page 82).

4. Do a facility/activity access check by phone or in person before going to an event with a person with a physical disability. This takes some practice. See Accessibility (page 103).

5. Do NOT overprotect or limit choices.

6. DO oversee safety needs.

Visual Impairments

Vision impairment covers the broad range of problems from what is called partial vision to total blindness. Anyone with a visual acuity in the better eye of 20/200 or less after correction is considered legally blind. Partial vision begins at 20/70 (Adams & McCubbin). Visual Impairments may result in other problems—such as lack of body control, static balance or poor coordination. There are many types of visual impairments and a variety of causes. Most people who are defined as blind actually can see, somewhat, either shadows or light. Many people with visual impairments do not use Braille.

Helpful Hints:

1. Do not yell, individuals with visual impairments are not hard of hearing.

2. Provide instructions in a multimodal manner using voice, touch, and/or coactive movement. See Communication (page 64).

3. Orientation is a key to comfort. Walk, talk, and allow the consumer with a vision impairment to feel his/her way around the facility.

4. The lighting condition of an area is important for full use of available vision. As each type of vision problem is different, consult with the person about what lights works best for him/her.

5. When assisting a person or guiding them, it is important to OFFER AN ELBOW. The person grabs the elbow as they wish and follows. Do not push or pull the person. A slight pause before steps and/or curbs with an explanation of the situation is helpful.

6. Guide dogs are working dogs, not fun and frolic pets to be played with and petted. Many people when approaching a person with a guide dog, talk to and interact with the dog while ignoring the person. This is disrespectful. Talk to the person, not the dog.

7. Safety hazards and emergencies may not be seen well by a person with visual impairments and must be dealt with in a think ahead manner.

8. Tandem is a common adaptation in biking, skiing, walking, running, canoeing, and other leisure activities.

9. Various kinds of adaptive equipment such as beeper balls and targets, and a variety of digital-computerized talking computers, and calculators is available to assist in participation. See Resources (page 145).

10. **Think Tactile!** Program activities can be enhanced with the incorporation of models, raised maps or diagrams, and boundaries of areas using masking tape, string, trailing guides, or changes in textures.

11. **Think Sound!** A bell, whistle, rattle, or voice can identify many objects or targets.

12. **Think Smell!** Yes, many visual experiences can be made into olfactory experiences. For instance, a small amount of scent or flavoring can be added to paints to allow a person to identify colors with a scent. Persons who have both visual and hearing impairments may know you by a cologne, so stick with one scent.

13. Think concrete spatial relations. Up, down, big, small, and distances are hard to define to someone who does not see. A person

who has blindness will probably not know what is meant by the statement that a steep hill is on the horizon, when cross-country skiing. Have a mutually determined code for stopping distances.

14. Hands-on is often the best way to teach a person a leisure skill. Try teaching golf just with your voice. Try teaching it by watching it. NOW, try teaching it by touch. Ask the learner if they would like to feel your golf position and if they agree, guide them to touch your shoulders, hands, knees and feet in brief intervals (five seconds each) in order to get the total picture. See *Do With Me Communication* (page 68).

15. Use your voice to help them see and don't be afraid to say . . . "Did you see that!", "Look over there!", or any sight related language.

A Special Note On Individuals Who Are Older

Generally speaking, the U.S. government classifies old age as beginning at 65. As we know, a person's physical, mental, and emotional status may vary greatly throughout life. Age in itself is not a disease or disability; however, older people may have impairments and disabilities due to a chronic illness such as heart disease, arthritis, and diabetes. One should not assume that old age means decline, disease, or disability. Some people are seen as old at 40 years of age while others are young at 90. If an older person has a disability, they are covered by the ADA.

Helpful Hints:

1. RESPECT is critical. You'll want to honor the person as someone with much experience and knowledge. The image of the older person as frail and being in a second childhood is OUT.

2. As people age, hearing and vision may decline. Denial of this often prohibits an older person from seeking medical attention (especially with hearing loss). Be sure the person is close, in front and has good lighting available for instructions, programs, and events. Just because a person is older, it is not necessary to assume hearing loss. Many older people resent being yelled at by those who assume there is hearing loss. See Hearing Impairments (page 132), and Visual Impairments (page 139).

3. Diet may be of concern due to diabetes, heart, and/or cholesterol problems. Sugar, salt and saturated fats are probably not a good idea. Refreshments of fresh fruit, crackers and yoghurt dips as opposed to sticky, sugary, greasy donuts are called for. If a sweet like ice cream is called for, make sure a comparable substitute like sugar-free ice cream is available.

4. Some older people have physical limitations or pain due to arthritis or other disease. See Wheelchairs and Devices (page 82).

5. Some older people like younger people, may have emotional problems. See Mental Health Problems (page 135).

6. Some older persons have cognitive difficulties like dementia or Alzheimer's disease. See Working and Playing With Indivivals With Learning Differences (page 81).

Resources Utilized
In Disability Categories Section

Adams, R. & McCubbin, J. (1991). *Games, sports and exercises for the physically disabled (4th ed.).* Malvern, PA: Lea & Febiger.

Austin, D. (1991). *Therapeutic recreation: Processes and techniques (2nd ed.).* Champaigne, IL: Sagamore Publishing Company.

Austin, D., & Crawford, M. (1991). *Therapeutic recreation.* Englewood Cliffs, NJ: Prentice-Hall.

American Diabetes Association. (1987). Nutrition and noninsulin dependent diabetes, Nutrition and insulin-dependent diabetes. Alexandria, VA: American Diabetes Association.

Beirsdorfer, W. (1991). *The student with hemophilia: A resource for the educator.* New York, NY: National Hemophilia Foundation.

Goldenson, R. (Ed.) (1978). *Disability and Rehabilitation Handbook.* Highston, NJ: McGraw Hill Books.

Grossman, H. J. (Ed.) (1983). *Classification in mental retardation.* Washington, D.C.: American Association of Mental Deficiency.

Grossman, H.J. (Ed.) (1990). *What young people should know about AIDS.* S. Deerfield, MA: Channing Bete Co. (Scriptographic Booklet).

National Hemophilia Foundation. (1990). *The child with hemophilia: First aid in school.* New York, NY: National Hemophilia Foundation.

Project LIFE. (1988). *LIFE resource manual.* Chapel Hill, NC: Center for Recreation and Disability Studies.

7

Resources

The last section! but useful. Important information found inside:

- Resources

- ADA Specific Resources

- Agencies for Networking

- Equipment and Assistive Devices

- Activity Directory and Resource Guide

- Americans with Disabilities Act Requirements Fact Sheet from the Department of Justice

Resources

The resources to assist in ADA compliance are diverse. They differ from region to region. The following lists are generic. Find a more specific list for your area and location. Try calling your State Parks and Recreation Society.

Look for consumers, speakers, organizations, equipment, transportation assistance, auxiliary aides such as sign language interpreters, and additional staff and volunteers, training tools such as books, tapes and sources of technical assistance.

ADA Specific Resources

The AMERICANS WITH DISABILITIES ACT OF 1990, Public Law 101-336, 101st Congress. July 26, 1990. Title II State and Local Government Services, published in the *Federal Register.* February 28, 1991. 28 CFR Part 35. Order No.1474-91. Title III Public Accommodations and Commercial Facilities published in the *Federal Register* February 22, 1991. 28 CFR Part 36. Order No.1472-91. The final rules on accessibility were issued by ATBCB July 26, 1991 in the *Federal Register*, CFR Part 1191. Contact:

Office on the Americans with Disabilities Act
U.S. Department of Justice, Civil Rights Division
P.O. Box 66118, Washington, DC 20035-6118

DOJ Hotline: Voice—(202) 514-0301; TDD—(202) 514-0381;
Electronic Bulletin Board—(202) 514-6193

Architectural Transportation Barriers Compliance Board (ATBCB)— Better known as the ACCESS Board, this agency regulates access in federally-funded facilities and helped create the ADA accessibility guidelines (ADAAG). This agency has a wealth of access information including: retrofit (redesign) manuals and inspection checklists for buildings, an upcoming standard for children's accessibility, ADA Accessibility Guidelines for Title II and III, and the Access America Newsletter. They now have a technical support expert in the area of recreation and park facilities.

USATBCB
1331 F. Street Suite 1000
NW Washington, DC 20004-1111

Phones: Voice—(800) 872-2253; TDD—(202) 272-5449;
FAX—(202) 272-5447

Uniform Federal Accessibility Standards (UFAS) can be obtained at no charge from ATBCB. See above address.

Technical Assistance Projects for ADA Compliance

These projects were supported by grant funds therefore the costs for products are usually nominal.

Communications Disabilities and ADA

A technical assistance project for Title II and Title III of ADA to assist in enhancing accessible communications. Includes (1) *Fact Sheets*—(a) *Communication and the ADA*, and (b) *Communication Disabilities*; and (2) video training materials. Contact:

American Speech-Language-Hearing Association
10801 Rockville Pike
Rockville, MD 20852

Phones: Voice/TDD—(800) 632-8255; Voice—(301) 897-5700;
TDD—(301) 897-0157; FAX—(301) 571-0457

National Center on Accessibility: Recreation, Parks, and Tourism

Center primarily focuses on accessibility related to park, recreation and hospitality/tourism. Research, training, materials and technical assistance via Technical Assistance Line are provided. Contact:

National Center on Accessibility
5040 State Road 67 North
Martinville, IN 46151

Phones: Voice/TDD—(800) 424-1877; or FAX—(317) 349-1086

Access Equals Opportunity: Your Guide to the Americans With Disabilities Act

This series of six booklets includes: Restaurants and Bars, Grocery Stores, Retail Stores, Fun and Fitness Centers, Car Sales and Service, and Medical Offices. Available from:

Council of Better Business Bureau's Foundation
4200 Wilson Boulevard
Arlington, VA 22203

Phone: (703) 247-3656

Several other grant-funded training and technical support grants related to the ADA are underway. Please contact the DOJ for a grantee list. The materials could be valuable to YOU!

Books on the ADA and Recreation

The ADA Self-Evaluation Handbook for Park Districts

Written by John McGovern (a lawyer and recreation administrator!), this handbook is available from:

National Parks and Recreation Association
2775 South Quincy Street Suite 300
Arlington, VA 22206-2204
Phone: (703) 820-4940

The Americans with Disabilities Act Resource Catalogue

Products related to attitude, education employment, housing, and transportation. Available from:

National Easter Seal Society
70 East Lake Street
Chicago, IL 60601

ADA Resource Guide for Parks, Recreation and Leisure Service Agencies

Written by E. Casciotti (1993), this guide lists consultants, current literature, funding and grant sources. Published by the National Parks and Recreation Association (See NRPA address, page148).

Agencies For Networking

The phone book has a section of social services, usually set apart and on a different color paper. Community guides to services are often available from United Way, Easter Seals, or another agencies. Call the public library.

These organizations are a good start because they deal with a variety of disabilities and are diverse in their goals. Exact titles of agencies/associations will vary from location to location:

- Governor's or Mayor's Committee on Employment of the Handicapped
- Independent Living Center
- Department of Rehabilitation
- Disability Resource and Referral Center
- City, County, or Area Committee on Persons with Disabilities and/or ADA
- National Handicapped Sports Association
- State Department of Social Services
- State Department of Health
- State Department of Human Services

The following agencies usually deal with a *specific disability*:

Office of Developmental Disabilities

Department of Special Education

Department of Mental Health

Area Office on Aging

United Way of America

Easter Seal Society

Association for Retarded Citizens (ARC)

United Cerebral Palsy Association

American Foundation for the Blind

AIDS Education/Resource Center

Regional Center for Developmental Disabilities

Deaf-Blind Regional Center

Head Injury Foundation

Center for the Hearing Impaired

There are foundations, associations, or societies for every type of disability group from cerebral palsy and multiple sclerosis to dyslexia. Search for local, state and national chapters/offices.

Equipment and Assistive Devices

Write or call for catalogues:

ABLEDATA—Adaptive Equipment Center

A wide variety of resources.

c/o *Newington Childrens' Hospital*
181 East Cedar Street
Newington, CT 16111

Phones: (800) 344-5405; TDD—(203) 667-5405

Adaptive Clothing

Special Clothes for Special People
P.O. Box 4220
Alexandria, VA 22303

Phone: (703) 549-2640

Adaptive Toys

Special Toys 4 Special Kids
11834 Wyandot Circle
Westminster, CO 80234

TherAdapt Products, Inc.
17 West 163 Oak Lane
Bensenville, IL 60106

Phone: (312) 834-2461

American Foundation for the Blind

Catalogue of adaptive devices including games and leisure equipment.

American Foundation for the Blind
15 West 16th Street
New York, NY 10011

Books in Large Print/Braille

American Printing House for the Blind, Inc.
1839 Frankfort Avenue
P.O. Box 6085
Louisville, KY 40206-0085

Phone: (502) 895-2405

Cassette Books Catalogue

Books on audio tape.

c/o CMLS
P.O. Box 9150
Melbourne, FL 32902

Things From Bell Recreation

Recreation equipment, some adaptive.

c/o Bell Recreation
230 Mechanic Street
Princeton, WI 54968

After Therapy Catalogue

Adaptive equipment for leisure and home living.

c/o *Access To Recreation Inc.*
2509 East Thousand Oaks Blvd Suite 430
Thousand Oaks, CA 91362

Phone: (800) 634-4351

Don Crebs' Access To Recreation

Adaptive equipment for physically challenged.

Access to Recreation
2509 E. Thousand Oaks Boulevard
Suite 430
Thousand Oaks, CA 91362

Phones: Toll Free—(800) 634-4351
International calls—(805) 498-7535

Communication Aids Catalog

Variety of assistive devices, electrical switchers and toys.

Crestwood Company
6625 N. Sidney Place
Milwaukee, WI 53209

Phone: (414) 352 5678

Sport Time

Physical education, dance and sport equipment. Some adaptives.

Sport Time
One Sportime Way
Atlanta, GA 30340

Phone: (800) 283-5700

The Specialists in Special Education

Programs for teaching sex education and social skills.

c/o James Stanfield Publishing Company
P.O. Box 41058
Santa Barbara, CA 93140

Phone: (800) 421-6534

Flaghouse Special Populations

Products for movement, play, and leisure.

c/o Flaghouse
150 N. MacQuesten Parkway
Mt Vernon, NY 10550

Phone: (800) 221-5185

The Play Factory

Play equipment and consultation.

The Play Factory
435-36th Street
Richmond, CA 94805

Phone: (415) 215-6243

Anyone Can Travel Resources

Accessibility listings and consultation.

Ms. Liz Cartwright
City of San Jose
Recreation Services
Office of Therapeutic Services
1500 Blossom Hill Road
San Jose, CA 95118

Phone: (408) 267-0200

Kids On The Block, Inc.

Puppets and skits for disability awareness training.

Kids On The Block, Inc.
9385-C Gerwig Lane
Columbia, MD 21046

Phone: (800) 368-KIDS

The International Directory of Recreation-Oriented Assistive Device Sources

Adaptive equipment.

c/o Lifeboat Press
P.O. Box 11782
Marina Del Rey, CA 90295

Activity Directory and Resource Guide

The following three pages are reprinted with permission of National Recreation and Parks Association, Northeast Regional Director, 1800 Silas Deanne Highway, Suite 1, Rocky Hill, CT 06067 from PIN–Vol 3#3 Celebrating Fun For Everyone T.R. Edition. (1991). *Programming From A to Z.* pp. 16-18.

Activity Directory

 Aerobics/Physical Fitness:
National Handicapped Sports and
    Recreation Association
1145 19th Street, N.W., Suite 717
Washington, D.C. 20036
(301) 652-7505

 Archery:
Wheelchair Archery Sport Section/
    NWAA
1604 E. Pikes Peak Avenue
Colorado Springs, CO 80909
(719) 635-9300

 Basketball:
National Wheelchair Basketball
    Association
110 Seaton Bldg.
University of Kentucky
Lexington, KY 40506
(606) 257-1623

 Bowling:
American Wheelchair Bowling
    Association
N54 W15858 Larkspur Lane
Menomonee Falls, WI 53051
(414) 781-6876

 Camping:
Office of Special Programs and
    Populations
National Park Service
U.S. Department of the Interior
P.O. Box 371127
Washington, D.C. 20013-7127
(202) 343-3674

 Fishing:
Fishing Fact Sheet
Outdoors Forever
P.O. Box 4811
East Lansing, MI 48826

 Football:
Recreation and Athletics
    Rehabilitation Education Center
University of Illinois
1207 South Oak Street
Champaign, IL 61820
(217) 333-4606

City of Santa Barbara
    Recreation Dept.
P.O. Drawer P-P
Santa Barbara, CA 93102
(805) 962-1474

 Golf:
Peter Longo
P.O. Box 27283
Tempe, AZ 85282
(602) 893-2092

John Klein
PGA Director of Golf
5830 Wolff Ct.
La Mesa, CA 92042
(619) 594-6699

 Horseback Riding:
North American Riding for the
    Handicapped Association
P.O. Box 33150
Denver, CO 80233
(303) 452-1212

 Kayaking:
Rick Ciccotto
2641 Cypress Gardens Road
Moncks Corner, SC 29461
(803) 761-2652

Nantahala Outdoor Center
Star Route, Box 68
Bryson City, NC 28713
(704) 488-2175

 Racquetball:
U.S. Wheelchair Racquet Sports
    Association/American Amateur
    Racquetball Association
1941 Viento Verano Drive
Diamond Bar, CA 91765
(714) 861-7312

 Road Racing:
Wheelchair Athletics of the
    USA/NWAA
1604 E. Pikes Peak Avenue
Colorado Springs, CO 80909
(719) 635-9300

 Rowing:
U.S. Rowing Association
Adaptive Racing Committee
11 Hall Place
Exeter, NH 03833
(603) 778-0315

 Sailing:
National Ocean Access Project
410 Severn Avenue, Suite 306
Annapolis, MD 21403
(301) 280-0464

Directory Continued

Scuba Diving:
Handicapped Scuba Association
1104 El Prado
San Clemente, CA 92672
(714) 498-6128

Skiing:
National Handicapped Sports
and Recreation Association
1145 19th Street, N.W., Suite 717
Washington, D.C. 20036
(301) 652-7505

Slalom:
Wheelchair Athletics of the
USA/NWAA
1604 E. Pikes Peak Avenue
Colorado Springs, CO 80909
(719) 635-9300

Softball:
National Wheelchair Softball
Association
P.O. Box 22478
Minneapolis, MN 55422
(612) 437-1792

Swimming:
Physically Challenged Swimmers
of America/NWAA
1604 E. Pikes Peak Avenue
Colorado Springs, CO 80909
(719) 635-9300

Table Tennis:
U.S. Wheelchair Table Tennis
Association/NWAA
1604 E. Pikes Peak Avenue
Colorado Springs, CO 80909
(719) 635-9300

Tennis:
National Foundation of
Wheelchair Tennis
940 Calle Amanecer, Suite B
San Clemente, CA 92672
(714) 361-2294

Track & Field:
Wheelchair Athletics of the
USA/NWAA
1604 E. Pikes Peak Avenue
Colorado Springs, CO 80909
(719) 635-9300

Weightlifting:
Wheelchair Athletics of the
USA/NWAA
1604 E. Pikes Peak Avenue
Colorado Springs, CO 80909
(719) 635-9300

Wilderness Activity Programs:
Blue Spruce Lodge/Guest Ranch
451 Marten Creek Road
Trout Creek, MT 59874
(406) 827-4762

Breckenridge Outdoor
Education Center
P.O. Box 697
Breckenridge, CO 80424
(303) 453-6422

Cooperative Wilderness Handicapped
Outdoor Group
Idaho State University
Box 8118
Pocatello, ID 83209
(208) 236-3912

Recreational Challenges
Box 442
Pierce, ID 83209
(208) 464-2118

Veterans of the Lake Wilderness Retreat
Star Route 1
Box 3420
Ely, MN 55731

Vinland National Center
P.O. Box 308
Loretto, MN 55357
(612) 479-3555

Voyageur Outward Bound School
10900 Cedar Lake Road
Minnetonka, MN 55343
(800) 328-2943 or (612) 542-9255

Wilderness Inquiry
1313 Fifth Street, S.E., Suite 327A
Minneapolis, MN 55414
(612) 379-3858

Resource Guide

BOOKS

Aquatics for Special Populations
YMCA Program Store, Box 5077, Champaign, IL 61820

Boating for the Handicapped
Human Resources Center, Albertson, NY 11507

Go For It!
Harcourt Brace Jovanovich, Orlando, FL 32887

A Guide to Recreation, Leisure and Travel for the Handicapped—Volume 1: Recreation & Sport
Resource Directories, 3103 Executive Parkway, Toledo, OH 43606

Interpretation for Disabled Visitors in the National Park System
Special Programs and Populations Branch, National Park Service, U.S. Department of the Interior, P.O. Box 371127, Washington, D.C. 20013-7127

The International Directory of Recreation-Oriented Assistive Device Sources
Lifeboat Press, P.O. Box 11782, Marina Del Rey, CA 90820

Playing & Coaching Wheelchair Basketball
University of Illinois Press,
54 E. Gregory Drive, Champaign, IL 61820
Phone: (800) 638-3030

Scuba Diving With Disabilities
Leisure Press, Box 5076, Champaign, IL 61820

Sports and Recreation for the Disabled: A Resource Manual
Benchmark Press, Inc., 8435 Keystone Crossing, Suite 175, Indianapolis, IN 46240

VIDEOTAPES

Challenge Golf (60 mins): 1/2" VHS and 3/4" U-Matic. Both a teaching version and a home-use version are available as an introduction to golf for people with disabilities. Contact Peter Longo at (602) 893-2092 for rental/sales information.

Fitness Is For Everyone (30 mins): 1/2" VHS or 3/4" U-Matic. A series of videotapes developed by the National Handicapped Sport and Recreation Association for improving aerobic fitness, physical strength and flexibility regardless of disability. For more information contact NHSRA or call (800) 468-2227.

Freedom In Depth (23 mins): 1/2" VHS, 3/4" U-Matic, or 16 mm film. An action-packed documentary featuring 19 divers who have disabilities in an underwater tour of southern California. Contact the Handicapped Scuba Association at (714) 498-6128 for rental/sales information.

Ocean Escapes (12 mins): 1/2" VHS. A beautifully produced video about scuba diving and individuals with disabilities. For more information, write to Ocean Escapes, P.O. Box 1969, Oceanside, CA 92051 or phone (800) 54SCUBA.

Go Beyond The Limits (28 mins): 1/2" VHS. A motivational tape showing hang gliding, off-road racing, sailing and glider flying, especially inspiring to the newly injured. For further information contact Everest & Jennings (Marketing Department) at (805) 987-6911.

Images In Excellence (9 mins): 1/2" VHS. Produced by the U.S. Olympic Committee, this videotape provides an introduction and brief overview of the wide range of competitive sports available for people with disabilities. Call the USOC Department of Library and Education Services at (719) 632-5551 to order the $10 tape.

Introduction To Wheeling And Long Distance Racing (37 mins): 1/2" VHS and 3/4" U-Matic. Equipment selection, accessories, techniques, training procedures and schedules are discussed with two top wheelers. Contact Vinland Center (612) 479-3555 for rental/sales information.

National Wheelchair Athletic Association Videotapes: 1/2" VHS. Coaching and training videos covering the popular NWAA sports of wheelchair racing, field/combined events, swimming, and table tennis. Call the NWAA at (719) 635-9300 for sales information.

Sit And Be Fit (30 min workout): 1/2" VHS. A scientifically designed workout to promote maximum health through aerobic workout and muscle conditioning. Call Sit And Be Fit at (602) 990-9005 for details.

Tennis In A Wheelchair (18 mins): 1/2" VHS and 3/4" U-Matic. A motivational tape designed to create interest, provide information and fundamental instruction in the basics of the game. Advanced instructional tape also available. Call the National Foundation of Wheelchair Tennis at (714) 361-2294 for sales information.

Wheelchair Basketball, Volumes I & II: 1/2" VHS. Developed by the authors of *Wheelchair Basketball*, these videos provide ideal team and group instruction and can be used with the text or as a valuable stand-alone instructional tool. Call PVA Sports at (800) 424-8200.

Video and Film Resources

A variety of films and videos are available that deal with issues concerning persons with disabilities. Focus on disability awareness themes for ADA training. Contact:

1. Local colleges and universities: Possible contacts include the instructional media center, Office of Students with Disabilities, therapeutic recreation departments, special education departments, psychology, physical or occupational therapy, or public administration departments.

2. Department of Rehabilitation: "A Different Approach" and others are recommended.

3. Governor's Committee on the Employment of the Handicapped

4. Regional Center for Developmentally Disabled

5. National Easter Seal Society

6. United Cerebral Palsy Association

7. National Handicapped Sports Association, local chapter

8. Any of the advocacy groups related to a specific disability such as the Foundation for the Blind or AIDS Resource center in your area.

9. Numerous public market films that portray issues related to disabilities are now available. Consider Rain Man, My Left Foot, Coming Home, One Flew Over the Cuckoo's Nest, Children of a Lesser God, Awakenings, and even, Edward Scissorhands, all have entertainment and educational values and can serve as a take-off point for discussion about attitudes and images of individuals with disabilities.

Books Related To Recreation Integration

Community Recreation and Persons With Disabilities: Strategies For Integration by Stuart J. Schleien and M. Tipton Ray. Paul Brookes Publishing Co, 1988. A practical how-to guide offering guidelines and model programs.

Special Recreation: Opportunities for Persons With Disabilities, 2nd ed. by Kennedy, Smith and Austin. WCB Publishers, 1991. Text focuses on community recreation and special populations. Both leadership and administrative concerns are covered.

LIFE (Leisure Is For Everyone) Project. Training program for community recreation professionals about persons with disabilities. Includes reasonably-priced manuals and a videotape. By Center For Recreation and Disability Studies, Leisure Studies, CB #8145, 730 Airport Road, Suite 204, University of North Carolina—Chapel Hill, Chapel Hill, NC 27599-8145 (919) 962-0534.

Park Access Digest by Whole Access, 517 Lincoln Avenue, Redwood City, CA 94061. Phone (415) 363-2647. A regular digest focused on access issues.

Recreation . . . Access in the 90s by NRPA. *A bimonthly newsletter providing information on the ADA, integration and accessibility.*

PIN, Programmers Information Network, Vol. 3, No. 3 ACTIVITY DIRECTORY by NRPA and Challenges Unlimited. Lists numerous organizations related to adaptive sports and activities from aerobics, scuba diving to tennis as well as an extensive book and video list.

Journal of Therapeutic Recreation. NRPA Publications. *This journal often has articles pertinent to integration.* National Recreation and Parks Association Publications, 2775 Quincy Street South, Suite 300, Alexandria, VA 22206-2204. Phone: (703) 820-4940.

Designing Guide for Accessible Outdoor Recreation—Interim Draft. Available from California Park and Recreation Society (CPRS), P.O. Box 161118, 3031 F Street, Suite 202, Sacramento. CA 95816. Phone: (916) 446-2777.

Golf and the ADA: A Winning Twosome Guidebook. The Summit Group, 1227 West Magnolia, Suite 500, Fort Worth, TX 76104. Phone: (800) 875-3346

Journal of Leisurability, Box 36, Station A, Islington, Ontario M9A 4X1, Canada. This journal focuses on integration issues.

IMPACT—A quarterly newsletter focusing on integration and main-streaming issues. Fall 1989 featured Recreation Integration Institute on Community Integration, 6 Pattee Hall, University of Minnesota, MLPS, MN 55455.

Together Successfully—Written by J. Rynders, Ph.D., and S. Schleien, Ph.D. (1991), topics include creating recreational and educational pro-grams that integrate people with and without disabilities. Includes practical guidelines for promoting integration from peer and staff train-ing viewpoints. Write to The National Association for Retarded Citizens, P.O. Box 1047, Arlington, TX 76004.

Inclusive Recreation: Planning Recreation Opportunities for People with All Abilities—(1992) Overview of various supporting leg-islation followed by practical suggestion for the implementation of inte-gration strategies. Contact the Michigan Department of Natural Re-sources, Recreation Services Division, Cynthia Burkhour, M.A., 2454 Lamplighter Drive, Jenison, MI 49428.

Creative Dramatics for an Integrated Group: Persons With and Without Disabilities— Step-by-step guidelines for development of an integrated community theatre program. Contact Awake-In-Dreams, Inc., 13863 Highland Drive, Grass Valley, CA 95945 or call (916) 272-1975.

Tennis for People With Differing Abilities Manual—A practical how-to guide to teaching tennis to indiviuals with disabilities. Write to HERO, 447 Ridge Road, Hartsdale, NY 10530, or phone (914) 946-6957 or (914) 347-5634.

The JOY of Signing [by L. Riekehop (1987) 2nd ed.] and *The JOY of Signing Puzzle Book* [by L. Hillebrand & L. Riekehof (1989)—*Joy of Signing* is great book to teach sign language with (which is also avail-able on videotape)! The puzzle book is a fun game book to motivate sign language learning. Both available from Gospel Publishing House, Springfield, MO 65802-1894.

People Resources

Recreation Therapists: Contact your State Parks and Recreation Society Therapeutic Recreation Board or Section. They usually have a directory of individuals who are members. Local recreation districts may also have a therapeutic recreation department. Call them!

Certified Therapeutic Recreation Specialists (CTRSs): Therapeutic recreation specialists are certified currently by NCTRC on the national level in the U.S. A directory of certified recreation specialists is available by contacting: NCTRC, 49 S. Main St., Suite 011, Spring Valley, NY 10977. Phone (914) 947-9660

Several States also have certification or licensing processes separate from National certification. Contact the State Parks and Recreation Society for referral to the correct certifying agency and their registry.

Staff and Volunteers: Be creative! Contact dance studios or the local college dance department to locate dance instructors. Call upon a media intern for help in public relations. Resources for volunteers and staff include:

1. Colleges, Universities, and High Schools

2. Volunteer Action Centers or Referral Agencies

3. Corporate Volunteer Programs

4. Charitable Organizations

5. Fraternities and Sororities

6. Community Service Sentences from the Courts

7. Work Training Participants

8. Consumers

9. Clubs and Groups such as Boys/Girls Clubs or Boy/Girl Scouts.

Consultants

Consultants are available to assist with ADA compliance. Be sure they fit the organization's needs. Recreation therapists, staff development specialists, lawyers and architects could be contracted for short term or on-going valuable assistance. Be sure they are qualified and have real-life working knowledge of ADA, integration and the functions of a recreation and leisure setting resembling the one you work at.

The following list of consultants are people that have influenced the development of this manual. They have a wide variety of skills in the area of integrated community based recreation and leisure programs and services.

1. Dr. John McGovern, CTRS: Executive Director, Northern Suburban Special Recreation Association, New Tier West Center, 7 Happ Road, Northfield, IL 60193. Phone (708) 501-4332. John is a recreation therapist, parks and recreation administrator and a lawyer, and the author of the ADA Self-Evaluation Handbook for Park Districts.

2. Dr. Carol Stensrud, CTRS, RTR. Stensrud is experienced in the development and implementation of integrated community-based leisure services and is the primary author of this book. She is the Director of LEISURANCE Associates, 372 Florin Road, Suite 236, Sacramento, CA 95831, a private consultation and training firm and an associate professor in recreation and leisure studies. Phone (916) 278-5668 or (916) 852-7288.

3. Ms. Terry Murray, A.P.E.: Murray, also of the LEISURANCE Associates Team, is a contributing author of this book, and specializes in adaptive sports and games. Phone (707) 425-2525

4. Ms. Sharon Adams, R.T.R.: Adams is also a contributing author of this book and a pioneer in supportive and adaptive recreation. She is also a member of the LEISURANCE Associates Team. Phone (916) 944-8673.

Stensrud, Murray and Adams regularly present training sessions, workshops and at conferences.

U.S Department of Justice
Civil Rights Division
Coordination and Review Section

Americans With Disabilities Act Requirements Fact Sheet

Employment

- Employers may not discriminate against an individual with a disability in hiring or promotion if the person is otherwise qualified for the job.

- Employers can ask about one's ability to perform a job, but cannot inquire if someone has a disability or subject a person to tests that tend to screen out people with disabilities.

- Employers will need to provide "reasonable accommodation" to individuals with disabilities. This includes steps such as job restructuring and modification of equipment.

- Employers do not need to provide accommodations that impose an "undue hardship" on business operations.

Who needs to comply:

- All employers with 25 or more employees must comply, effective July 26, 1992.

- All employers with 15-24 employees must comply, effective July 26, 1994.

Transportation

- New public transit buses ordered after August 26, 1990 must be accessible to individuals with disabilities.

- Transit authorities must provide comparable paratransit or other special transportation services to individuals with disabilities who cannot use fixed route bus services, unless an undue burden would result.

- Existing rail systems must have one accessible car per train by July 26, 1995.

- New rail cars ordered after August 26, 1990 must be accessible.

- New bus and train stations must be accessible.

- Key stations in rapid, light, and commuter rail systems must be made accessible by July 26, 1993 with extensions up to 20 years for commuter rail (30 years for rapid and light rail).

- All existing Amtrak stations must be accessible by July 26, 2010.

Public Accommodations

- Private entities such as restaurants, hotels, and retail stores may not discriminated against individuals with disabilities, effective January 26, 1992.

- Auxiliary aids and services must be provided to individuals with vision or hearing impairments or other individuals with disabilities, unless an undue burden would result.

- Physical barriers in existing facilities must be removed, if removal is readily achievable. If not, alternative methods of providing the services must be offered, if they are readily achievable.

- All new construction and alterations of facilities must be accessible.

State and Local Government

- State and local governments may not discriminate against qualified individuals with disabilities.

- All government facilities, services, and communications must be accessible consistent with the requirements of section 504 of the Rehabilitation Act of 1973.

Telecommunication

- Companies offering telephone service to the general public must offer telephone relay services to individuals who use telecommunications devices for the deaf (TDDs) or similar devices.

The ADA Fact Sheet is available in the following accessible formats:

* Braille

* Large print

* Audio tape

* Electronic file on computer disk and electronic bulletin board. (202) 514-6193

For more information about the ADA contact:

U.S. Department of Justice
Civil Rights Division
Coordination and Review Section
P.O. Box 66118
Washington, DC 20035-6118

(202) 514-0301 (Voice); (202) 514-0381 (TDD); (202) 514-0383 (TDD)

CRD-20
GPO: 1990 0-273-184